I Survived. Now What? Finding Meaning From Loss.

Jerry L. Cook, Ph.D., C.F.L.E.

I Survived. Now What? Finding Meaning From Loss.

Jerry L. Cook, Ph.D., C.F.L.E.

Also by Dr. Jerry L. Cook:

The Parents' Guide to Raising CEO Kids

The 10 Minute Marriage Manager: Daily Maintenance for Couples on the Grow

The Prodigal Son

Grow Your Marriage by Leaps and Boundaries

DISCLAIMER: This book is designed for educational purposes and cannot guarantee a particular benefit.

ISBN-10: 0-9836880-0-1
ISBN-13: 978-0-9836880-0-6

Printed in the United States of America

Acknowledgements

Dedicated to Mom (b. 1942- d. 1985).

A special debt of gratitude is in my heart for everyone who bravely shared their stories of loss and potential. Thank you for your courage and inspiration.

I also appreciate University Enterprise Inc. at California State University, Sacramento, whose funds helped me write this book.

Acknowledgements...iv

Preface ix

Chapter 1: Introduction 2

Chapter 2: Know Your Loss 7

    The Concept of Loss 9

    Your Loss Baseline...13

    The Language of Loss...18

Chapter 3: The Potential Framework.......................................23

Chapter 4: To Feel Safe Again 33

    Unsafe Triggers 35

    Changing Our Thoughts About The Lack of Safety 37

    To Fear or Not to Fear 38

    Scarcity and Reframing 43

    The Target Always Changes and is Never Good Enough......46

    To Trust Again...47

    Types of Trust...53

    Safety and Trust Antagonists 55

    Recharging the Batteries for Introverts............................58

    If Safety is Unlikely...59

Chapter 5: Influence 64

    Parenting 65

    Wanting to Influence, Yet Feeling Restricted.....................66

    Singing...69

    Sharing Your Voice in Creative Ways................................70

"I'm There For You" 73

Feeling Stuck 74

Complaining 76

Inner Critical Voices 78

Humor 80

Talents 82

Being Influential Doesn't Mean Influencing Everyone 83

Chapter 6: Value 86

Self-Talking 87

Changing Your Thoughts About Your Value 89

Valuing Your Loss 90

Seeds of Change 90

The Self-Esteem Myth 93

Tying Your Value to Things That Last 94

Children's TV Programming 94

Your Value, Alone 95

Chapter 7: Investment 99

Recalling the Potential Framework 100

The Danger of Not Investing 100

Investing as Parents 102

Investing in Others 103

Simple Acts of Investing 104

Altruism 107

Investment Priorities and Balancing 108

Investment Careers 110

Chapter 8: Acceptance and the Power of Letting Go 113

Why Acceptance Fuels Future Perceptions..........................115

Perfectionists 119

Gratitude 122

Adapting 124

Forgiveness...127

Forgiving Yourself..131

A Whole New Level 131

This isn't What Life is All About 132

Chapter 9: Potential Revisited 137

Having Your Best Day Ever 137

Increasing Our Potential Never Means Pushing Others Down 141

Do I Take Care of Me First or is That Selfish?...................142

Pet Loss..143

Metamorphosis 145

Run the Race..146

Mental Illness 147

Love..149

Morality 150

A "Potential" Table and Summary 151

The Potential Framework...152

Affirmations...153

Chapter 10: Limitations and Exceptions 156

Semantics...157

For the Academic and Practitioner 158

Chapter 11: Help and Hope 165

Chapter 12: Conclusion..169

Helping Others Reach Their Potential 170

Chapter 13: Epilogue 171

Preface

I was having a really bad day. My "work day" had ended and I took all of my frustrations to a local grocery store. It was there I noticed a man who had finished shopping and was exiting the store. He had two prosthetic legs, and while holding two bags of groceries, he hopped onto his bicycle and pedaled away.

That moment and many others like it have impressed upon me the need to write this book. The process was long, but rewarding, as I collected accounts from those who have experienced loss and trauma and yet have thrived in the face of adversity. How do they do it? How can they live emotionally rich lives when life has not treated them well? Drawing upon the interviews of victims, survivors, and experts, this book provides the answers.

We all share in the life of loss, and we can help one another cope, survive, and develop greater value because of that loss. The stories shared with me have changed my life for the better, and I have witnessed the impact they have had on others. I wish I could have written about everyone who shared their story with me, but the process of writing a book requires hard choices regarding which stories are published and which are not. I hope everyone who participated in this remarkable process knows I greatly appreciate their kindness and courage.

There are two ideal options for reading this book. The first is to stop after each chapter, and to take some time applying what you have learned, before reading the next chapter. The second option is to read through the book, cover to cover, with the goal of understanding the overall principles, and then returning to those areas you feel most connected with. The first approach will lead to a slow-but-steady, more structured, path for improvement, while the second provides the reader with a self-selected route for identifying areas for improvement.

May you experience hope, healing, and success in the journey ahead.

Jerry

Section 1

Chapter 1: Introduction

"Loss" is more of an experience than an event.

If you have experienced a loss in your life, you know that the aftershocks of a traumatic event can be as devastating as the event itself. Whether we experience the loss of health, the loss of a loved one, or a loss of hope, loss follows us wherever we go and with whatever we do. It affects our judgment, our ability to trust, and our willingness to take risks. Although the concept of loss will be expanded throughout these pages, this book is for you if you feel a loss, or "at a loss," over a traumatic event or following chronic negative experiences.

Loss affects our relationships, our work, and our health. Those who suffer the most from loss often feel at least one of the following: (1) A loss of control or influence over one's life, (2) A loss of one self (or confusion about who they really are), and (3) Difficulty reconnecting with people and things that were important to them prior to the loss.

I have spent hundreds of hours conducting research, and more importantly, interviewing those who had experienced loss and trauma. Initially, my goal for this book was to help individuals and families cope with loss. I was motivated to learn what "got them through," how they endured, almost like being able to indefinitely cling to a rope over a steep cliff. But as the process continued, and particularly as I interviewed more and more people, I became amazed with the real life accounts of how pain and loss morphed into the fuel for becoming and doing incredible things. This book addresses that pain and trauma, but it focuses much more

2

on the answer to, "Now what do I do now that I've survived?" It also gives an affirmative answer to, "What if the things causing us the most heartache and pain can make us whole and stronger than before?" More importantly, these pages show you how. This book is about change and improvement, but it's different than many self-improvement books because it's based on science, experts in the field, research, and most importantly, person-proven strategies to help you connect the dots between where you are and where you can be.

In this section of the book, we'll start by looking at what "loss" is. It may seem like a very simple word, but it is actually quite complex.

Talking about loss is difficult for a lot of people. And yet there is a danger in not being able to talk about something that is so hurtful. The quality of our lives is dependent on being able to understand, work with, and make meaning from the loss in our lives.

Life goes on after loss, even if we seemingly cannot go on with it. When others ask us how we are doing, we automatically know we should say we are doing fine, even when we're not doing well.

Loss victims and survivors often hear and feel the echoes of the past in their thoughts, relationships, and in many of their decisions. Everywhere they go there are triggers to bring back the memories of that loss, including birthdays, anniversaries, certain foods, words, scents, and even what some people look like.

This book is designed to help loss victims and survivors find their voice, and at times, for this book to be their voice, in order to find their motivation for truly living. It is not about getting revenge or justice, although there is that temptation for many who experience loss. Instead, this book is designed to help you expand and reach your potential by meeting your own needs, as well as expanding your ability to help others in need.

While many loss victims feel that no one wants to hear about their loss, some who have experienced loss and trauma are repeatedly asked to revisit their pain. They are viewed as their disease, their inabilities, and their loss. Some may even be judgmental of you if you try to be happy through your loss.

> *In times of struggle or heartache, we tend to be blinded by the challenges at hand and miss the positive and special experiences we should have gratitude for. Many people throughout my life have faulted me for having a positive attitude and wrongly surmised that I have lived a life of bliss that can only be found in an episode of "The Andy Griffith Show." I wrote "White Lilies in Autumn" with the hope that I could show people that although we struggle with depression, loss, challenges and other problems, we can stand up, dust ourselves off, ask for help and move forward. --*
> -- Dustin Bradshaw

The first section of this book will introduce a new "Potential Framework" to illustrate concepts and principles of growth for the remaining chapters. The second section includes more details for each "stage" of the Potential Framework, and illustrates the process of change with stories from those I interviewed for this book. The final section looks at some of the challenges of the Potential Framework, and further explores how understanding your potential is important in a wide range of situations.

NOTES

Bradshaw, D. (2012). *White Lilies in Autumn.* Saratoga
Village, CA: American Book Publishing.

Chapter 2: Know Your Loss

As mentioned, "loss" can encompass many things. Understanding the common themes or threads across a diverse continuum of "loss" experiences will provide you with increased opportunities for connecting, reaching, and lifting others.

Assume for a minute you were listening to someone speak about their loss and they said, "I miss her. You know, I can't believe she's gone." What would you think of? Who would you think of? The reason "loss" is a universal experience is because what others experience means something to us. We remember our own loss, or we remember a loved one who experienced loss.

I think of my mom when I hear the words "She's gone." My mom died of cancer when I was 14. Others may envision their experience with a runaway child, a child who passes away, or the loss of custody following a divorce. Others may think of a spouse who left them, a child who moves away to go to college, or a friend who no longer wants anything to do with them.

Loss can be unexpected or expected, voluntary or involuntary, but it is always painful. Understanding the patterns of loss across diverse experiences and backgrounds is important if we are to move through our pain and help others manage their loss experience.

Of course, not all forms of loss are considered equal. However, there are common pathways for how we deal with loss, and understanding these commonalities is what helps us empathize with others.

The seeds of my interest in "loss" and its effects began at a very early age. Growing up on a farm, I was well aware of the beginning and end of life, and how the animals (and our livelihood) depended on how well we could limit early death, infection, or poor nutrition among them. But my first experience with someone close to me dying happened when I was in second grade, with a friend who had leukemia. Then, in my teen years, there were two male friends who each lost one of their parents; one friend seemed to be quite resilient from that loss, and the other friend struggled considerably. Later, in my young adult years, I worked extensively with men who had disabilities, from schizophrenia to Obsessive Compulsive Disorder to Down Syndrome. What troubled me most was how rare it was for their families, who lived just a few miles from them, would visit them, even over the phone. Not only were their disabilities a form of loss, but they had essentially lost their families.

Shortly after my work with men who had disabilities, I worked with juvenile delinquents, and realized that the innocence of childhood was lost, and their attempt at a "normal," healthy, future felt hopeless. I also worked with families in the housing projects of Nashville, Tennessee, and began to see how the cycle of poverty and the loss of hope were perpetuated.

As noted by Patrick Wanis, human behavior expert and celebrity life coach, loss is, "I can never ever have this again. I can never again have the benefits from what I have lost, what I no longer have, or what I can never have." Loss can also be felt with something you have never had, such as never having a positive childhood, enough money, or good health.

Despite loss and the challenges we all experience from that loss, this book proves that reaching one's potential and developing a sense of resilience is not only possible, but absolutely necessary, for our well-being. In research my wife and I conducted with gifted youth, we noticed that many of their talents were directly linked with how they handled their grief and pain; when they were able to develop a sense of purpose, hope, and direction from their loss and pain, they were much more resilient than those who tried to hide their pain. Such is the nature of this book.

The Concept of Loss

The source of *all* pain and suffering, whether physical, emotional, relational, or spiritual, is loss. Everyone loses something or someone that is important to them, and we all respond to loss in different ways. One thing is certain: Loss changes us. We can either be stronger and more compassionate because of that loss, or we can feel more lonely and afraid. We can live in continual fear and mistrust or live each moment with purpose and with great potential. There is no "normal" or going back to who we once were or what we once had. Although we cannot reclaim the past, many still try to live in the past, thinking if we did something differently, things would have turned out better.

There is an urgent need for understanding how to manage loss and the pain that comes from that loss. Pain and loss are huge expenses for our communities. Each has productivity costs, causing sick days and reduced work efficiency. There are vast social implications, as individuals unable to deal with pain and loss are at increased risk for hurting others, acting out what had been done to them, finding temporary solace in revenge. Hurt people tend to hurt people, destroying hopes, hearts, and childhood innocence. When pain and loss aren't dealt with in a positive way, a new plague is created with each new hurt person affecting even more people. The cycle of loss continues from one family or generation to the next.

The financial cost of pain for individual and family budgets is off the charts, with billions of dollars spent on medicine, supplements, unhealthy eating, obesity, and eating disorders, just to name a few. Pain and loss have an untold cost on relationships, marriages, and families, as those who are struggling with pain and loss also struggle with meeting the needs of those who depend on them.

We all know what pain is and what it feels like, but what exactly does "loss" refer to, and does it apply to you? Although the concept and definition of loss will be greatly expanded as you progress through the book, the simplest definition of loss is that something, or someone, is missing. It is also often an emotion, that something doesn't feel right, fixed, or resolved, especially following a traumatic or series of negative events.

If you have experienced any hardship, challenge, or trauma affecting how you think, feel, or form relationships with others, then you have experienced loss. It is the sense that an opportunity, dream, value, hope, or person you love, need, or want is gone.

If you are a survivor or victim of multiple loss experiences, it's difficult to find the right resources. A search online for books with the words "loss" will likely net you one of three categories: financial loss, death of a parent/loved one, and (ironically, a "loss" most people want) weight loss. Many of these resources can be helpful, but when you have experienced a series of negative loss events, you may need a resource covering a broader range of loss experiences.

Sometimes "loss" is tangible, direct, or obvious, such as the loss of health, the loss of a parent or child, a loss of employment, or a loss of a relationship. Intangible losses, such as an unfulfilled dream, loss of hope, or having a relationship that isn't what you had expected or needed it to be are much more common than tangible loss. Particularly with the intangible losses, we write them off as "Oh, it's just stress," giving loss an ambiguous label that masks the true source of that pain. Many times we don't even know what the source of that pain or stress is, but we feel its effects nonetheless.

This is particularly true for those who experience child loss. Most of the "child loss" literature focuses on parents who have lost their children to death or about parents struggling with the disability of their child, but I consider the category of "child loss" to be much more diverse. Many of us have experienced some kind of "loss" in childhood, either through our parents divorcing, the death of a parent, or the loss of a normal or healthy childhood. Most adults have some regret, fear, or "something missing" from their childhood, and most parents experience some level of loss as their child moves on, experiences trauma, or chooses their own path rather than following their parents' advice.

Whether your source of stress and pain is tangible or intangible, recent or lifelong, in your childhood or in adulthood, known or unknown, this book will help you learn more about how that loss impacts you. More importantly, you will identify strategies to make you stronger, more connected with those you care about, and someone you personally respect and appreciate.

What I will share with you is grounded in the stories of those I interviewed. It is also scientifically verifiable. Consider, for example, an interesting study titled, "Meeting risk with resilience: High daily life reward experience preserves mental health," where the authors had their participants complete several tasks, and assessed their depression and anxiety levels before and after the intervention. For the intervention, the participants were randomly notified via a wristwatch 50 times over a period of a week to fill out questionnaires regarding their current mood and how rewarding their most recent "major" event was. Not surprisingly, the results show that those who had more rewarding life events each day had less risk for mental health problems. However, these major, rewarding life and daily experiences were especially protective for those who had experienced childhood adversity. In the words of the study's authors, ". . . with increasing levels of childhood adversity, the protective effect of high reward experience became more pronounced."

Unfortunately, it is difficult knowing how to have these kinds of protective events when you do not feel well. I believe the answer to having protective life events is by building your potential.

Before addressing the process of potential, it is important to understand your "baseline," meaning where you are starting from before trying something new. Below is a list of events, experiences, and emotions reflecting different types of loss. Mark a "Y" for "yes" next to each item listed below for which you have experienced. If the item does not apply to you, do not mark it with anything.

I often wish one or more of my parents was/were nicer to me while I was growing up.

My parent(s) often made me feel shame or guilt for no reason.

I was kidnapped as a child.

I experienced a disability and/or a significant accident as a child.

I feel guilty about many things from my childhood.

I feel guilty about how my child is being raised.

As a child, I often felt responsible for my parents' emotions and how they reacted to me.

During my youth, I lost a relationship or person that was very important to me.

I frequently have thoughts about a relationship I wish I had as a child/teen, either with my parents, a dating partner, or a mentor.

I often feel that something in my childhood was missing.

I was bullied during my childhood.

My child has been kidnapped.

I felt unsafe in my childhood.

I rarely felt I could share my true self, feelings, or thoughts in my childhood.

I often forget things about my childhood I should remember.

I dislike remembering my childhood

I dislike talking about my childhood.

I feel guilty when talking about my childhood loss.

I experienced considerable pain or trauma in my childhood.

My child is deceased.

I often feel responsible for the pain my child experiences (or has experienced).

I have experienced infertility.

I have temporarily lost my child.

I have lost my child long-term.

I am often sad or angry because my child has not followed my recommendations or guidance.

My child is not as emotionally close to me as I would like.

My child has been bullied.

My parents are separated or divorced.

I have been divorced.

I often feel frustrated that what I say or do isn't appreciated.

I have experienced unwanted unemployment.

I felt (or feel) compelled to work in a place I did/do not like.

I have felt compelled to stay in a relationship I did not want to stay in.

I am often stressed about money.

Growing up, my parents were often stressed about money.

I grew up in poverty.

I grew up in an area where violence was common.

I am raising my child(ren) in an area or community that does not have the education or experience I want them to have.

I have experienced a "break-up" of a relationship that was very important to me.

I had to grow up quicker than I wanted to (or should have).

Painful thoughts or feelings from past memories affect my relationships with others.

My experience with loss makes it difficult to concentrate/focus.

It is difficult communicating with the opposite sex.

It is difficult communicating with those who remind me of my parents.

I find it difficult to trust or get as close to others as I'd like.

I experienced abuse in my childhood.

I have been abused as an adult.

I sometimes find myself manipulating others so they will depend more on me.

I am frequently manipulated by those closest to me.

I get nervous or stressed when others want to get to know the "real me."

I am often jealous of other people's backgrounds.

I struggle with whether I should feel close to those who have hurt me.

I struggle with forgiving those who hurt me during my childhood.

I was made fun of because of my looks, interests, talents, or speech.

I struggle with forgiving those who should have protected me during my childhood.

Others complain or tease me for "acting childish," silly, or immature.

Those I love frequently complain that my mind seems to be somewhere else.

I find myself distancing or avoiding those who remind me of getting hurt as a child.

I have been abandoned.

I feel a sense of emptiness in my life.

I experienced deprivation in my childhood.

My house was broken into or vandalized.

My car was stolen or vandalized.

Count up all the "yes" answers, and consider if you have been aware of how much loss you've experienced or its impact in your life. It is important to realize that this survey is not a formal or "scientific" survey, but rather showcases experiences, including events and effects, common among those who have experienced loss. Of course, if all forms of loss were available in the list, it would fill more than all the pages in this book. In sum, however, the greater the number, the more loss you have likely experienced and/or the greater its impact on your life. Of course, any loss, no matter the amount, can have an enormous impact on our lives.

The Language of Loss

The meaning of loss is a strong predictor for how we adapt after loss, trauma, or a crisis. Those who do not find meaning, or a positive meaning, for their loss often struggle with coping. If your loss event occurred years ago and you are still asking yourself why it happened to you, or worse, if you feel it is a "sign" or reflection of what you deserve, then you are less likely to move past your pain than the person who has found a positive meaning, or purpose, for that pain.

Although finding a positive meaning or interpretation of your pain is often a long journey, one place to begin is by understanding the Language of Loss. I designed the Language of Loss to help (1) loss victims understand what they were feeling and why they were feeling it, (2) validate their loss experience and pain from that loss, and (3) identify positive meaning from that loss.

Let's take a hypothetical example. Imagine that I was in a car wreck a year ago, and that my car was totaled and I had to take a few days off from work because I got whiplash. Shortly after, my health improved and the car repaired, and yet I still struggle (and perhaps obsess) with the thoughts of that accident. I might ask myself why I'm not "over it" by now, or wonder why it is still affecting me when everything has appeared to return to normal.

To understand what I was feeling, I would look at all my losses surrounding that accident. At first, this may seem quite obvious: loss of car function (or availability) and a loss of health because of an injury. But there is much more: I *lost* confidence in my driving which leads to *losing* trust that I can keep my passengers safe. Perhaps I *lost* control of my thoughts because each time I pass the place where I got in the accident, my mind can't stop thinking about it. Perhaps there is also a *loss* of trust for other drivers and I get incredibly anxious when driving around others. Or it may be that I have a *loss* of confidence, not only in driving, but also in other areas of my life (e.g. work, relationships, etc.) after my car wreck.

You can see from this hypothetical example that our loss *event* often consists of more than one loss *experiences*. Below is space for you to write down all the things you lost because of one of your loss events. Use the word "loss" or a variation of it (e.g. lost, losing, loses) in each of your answers below.

------------------------   ------------------------   ---------------

------------------------   ------------------------   ---------------

------------------------   ------------------------   ---------------

Sometimes it is difficult knowing exactly what was lost or why an event can have such a profound impact on us. An alternative approach (to the activity above) is to look at the changes that occurred after a traumatic moment, whether they are logically connected to our primary loss event or not. For example, perhaps after a car accident there is more conflict between me and my siblings, spouse, or children. Or it may seem that others are treating me harshly for no reason. Even if these changes are not directly related to my car wreck, they still happened shortly after my wreck.

Now it's your turn. List as many of these changes, especially the difficult or painful changes, that occurred after your loss in the area below. These changes may involve changes in other people, in your circumstances, or in you shortly after your loss. It may help if you said or thought the words, "Before the loss, (I/she/he/it) was" and then compare pre-loss with after the loss. List the negative changes below.

------------------------ ------------------------ ----------------

------------------------ ------------------------ ----------------

------------------------ ------------------------ ----------------

For many who begin to realize their loss experiences and its impact, it validates what they are feeling. This is because the loss provides meaning, something most people need before learning how to move on or press forward in life.

The final exercise involves understanding how our loss experience can make us better than we are now. In my earlier example of a car accident, instead of it making me less trusting, it *could* have made me more grateful for things and people. It could have helped me prioritize my schedule to make sure I spent more time with those I cared about. It could have motivated me to help others drive safer. I could save lives by doing that.

In the space below, consider how your loss (that you addressed above) could have improved your life. It may include what you could accomplish or it may involve a change in your personality, relationships, or skills. No matter how small or idealistic, list how your loss could have improved you, your life, or your relationships.

------------------------   ------------------------   ---------------

------------------------   ------------------------   ---------------

------------------------   ------------------------   ---------------

In this last exercise, you have determined what your potential after loss really is. You are also beginning to see how your loss experiences can make you stronger. Perhaps loss, trauma, or a crisis has held you back, but now you can choose how it will improve your life, as well as the life of others. Consider using these examples, or Language of Loss activities, for each of your loss events or experiences. (Note: It is strongly recommended that you take frequent breaks or let a professional help you through them if you experience any serious discomfort from these activities).

NOTES

Geschwind, N., Peeters, F., Jacobs, N., Delespaul, P., Derom, C., Thiery, E., van Os, J., & Wichers, M. (2010). Meeting risk with resilience: High daily life reward experience preserves mental health. *Acta Psychiatrica Scandinavica, 122,* 129-138.

Chapter 3: The Potential Framework

Thus far, we have focused primarily on the loss you have experienced, and how much of an impact it can have. If the bad news is how much destruction it can do (or has done) in your life, the flip side is from that experience you can become incredibly purposeful and resilient, and that you can help instill those gifts in others.

Our past, difficult experiences can no longer serve as valid reasons for our setbacks in life. Our emotions depend more on our perception than on the actual events, no matter how traumatic they are. This concept was illustrated in the book, *The Happiness Advantage*, by Shawn Achor, who demonstrates that our external circumstances do not determine our happiness. Achor presents a compelling case that what we have or what we have experienced is not as strong of a predictor for our well-being as the choices we make.

One of my favorite stories of people with great potential is Michael Oher, a professional football player portrayed in the movie *The Blind Side*. Michael lived part of his childhood life in homelessness and foster homes. His mother was addicted to drugs and his father wasn't around. In his book, *I Beat the Odds*, Michael explains how the very thing that others saw as a problem actually became his greatest asset. In the opinion of many experts and social workers, Michael (as a child) was too quiet, too shy, and they lamented about why he didn't open up more to others. But what others called "shy" was actually an enhanced ability to observe people and things.

In his teens, he realized that his powerful ability to observe, or observing other athletes, was his ticket to a better life. Using what others saw as a crutch became the mechanism for reaching his potential, and it is largely the reason why he is where he is today. Although opportunities came his way because of those who helped him, the reality is that his hidden talent of "observation" helped him take advantage of those opportunities in ways others would not have.

I was also very inspired by Anna Beninati, who learned that loss can often serve as the foundation for future triumphs. In her first few days at college, Anna went train hopping with some friends, slipped, and had her legs crushed by the moving train. All she could do was watch. As a bilateral amputee, Anna knows a great deal about loss, but found incredible strength because of that loss. Her response is motivational. "It occurs to me sometimes, I lived through this. There's nothing else I can't live through."

As noted from the Language of Loss, most who live with one form of loss usually need to learn to cope with a series of losses. For Anna, in addition to the loss of her legs, there was the emotional difficulty of having her family take care of her every need.

> *After I got home there was a ramp in my backyard, rails by the toilet and in the shower, and it really hit me, 'This is the rest of your life. This is not going to go away. It was hard'. For about a week, all I could do was wallow in self-pity. I was content to give up. Then one night, I knew that was no way to live. I could give up, but I had a lot of life ahead of me. After that, I made a mental effort to be more*

emotionally healthy. There was one time when I was
upstairs, and while I wasn't supervised by my mom,
I got out of my wheelchair and onto the floor, and
crawled downstairs to play video games for the first
time since the accident. And I thought, 'Oh my gosh,
look at what your body just did. What else are you
capable of?'

Your loss can inspire you to make powerful changes, but only if that loss is placed within the right context. For Anna, part of that context was finding accomplishment as a Paralympics skier.

I created the Potential Framework to help guide us through the rest of this book, and to use it as a way of better understanding and applying the advice given by those I interviewed. The framework consists of the following basic principles:

1.   Our potential increases as we transition through five stages (Safety, Influence, Value, Investment, and Acceptance).

2.   Our current potential is reduced when our ability to meet our needs becomes scarce.

3.   Our needs in our early years are initially met by caregivers, and if those needs are met, our needs become increasingly focused on helping others.

4.   If a need is not met in our childhood, it will permeate our thoughts, emotions, and actions until that need is met.

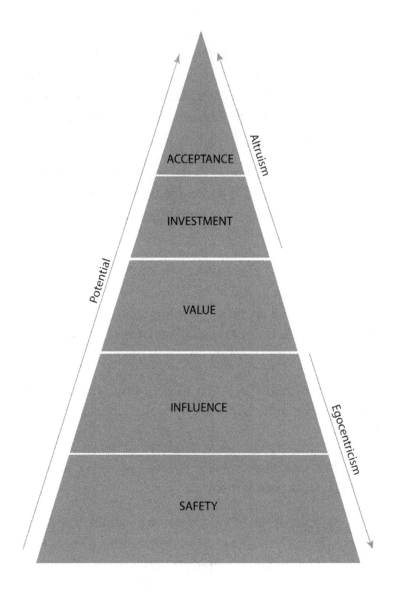

The Potential Framework is important for understanding loss because it identifies the needs of the victim/survivor, it indicates how and when a person's development may become "stuck," and it (re-)connects the victim/survivor to others by using their skills and experiences in a way that strengthens the giver and recipient. Helping someone who has experienced loss reach their potential is helping them move from feeling like they have to defend themselves from life to truly living life. In that context, understanding and reaching one's potential is one of the most compassionate things you can do for someone who has experienced loss, even if that person is you. Reaching your potential and helping others meet theirs are also consistent with the idea of building resilient individuals, families, and communities.

Some individuals are more motivated to reach their potential than others. Regardless of biology and other resources (or setbacks), there are steps each of us can take to make our loss a meaningful part of our lives, something that motivates and guides us to improve and help others. There is a drastic need for those who have experienced loss to find meaning and hope from that loss. There is an equal need for those who have experienced loss to use their hardship as a way for strengthening others. Each of us has a moral obligation to improve the lives of others, and our loss may give us the compassion and courage to help others discover their own potential.

I believe what drives each of us to change, improve, and dream is our inherent need to see, expand, and reach our potential. Our "potential" is the engine hidden under the hood that drives us to do the things we do. It is the reason we want to strengthen our relationships, to improve our finances, or to achieve our goals; more precisely, it is the reason we are motivated to do and be better than we are. Potential is that little grocery clerk in your head, asking, "Have you found everything you're looking for today?" We are literally made and programmed to be all we can be, and we will find the greatest comfort and satisfaction when we realize our potential.

I want to make it clear that the motivation to change, improve, and become isn't always a feel-good emotion. To the contrary, it is often one filled with need, "I have to," desperation, and frustration. Being frustrated was a very common reason many therapists and life coaches indicated as the primary motivator for their clients to seek professional help, and despite the discomfort of feeling frustrated, it has a powerful purpose.

> *Those who are ready (to succeed) quite often use the word "frustrated." They say they've had enough and they want to change. They're willing to go outside of their comfort zone.* --- Vironika Tugaleva, author, speaker, and life coach

One of the key elements for recognizing what is holding us back from our potential is being aware of our emotions or feelings. Daniel Goleman, author of *Emotional Intelligence*, states, "An inability to notice our true feelings leaves us at their mercy" (p. 43). And understanding our potential is all about recognizing how our emotions impact our lives, relationships, and decision making. As noted by Robert Brooks and Sam Goldstein, authors of The *Power of Resilience*, "Resilient people are not only aware of their feelings….they also take personal responsibility for change" (p. 31). This synchronous dance between being aware of our pain coupled with our commitment to forge that pain into something more positive is what potential is all about.

Being unaware of our emotions and needs is one of the surest ways for repeating history. We tend to be most sensitive to, yet least consciously aware of, our greatest needs, and we tend to develop unrealistic expectations for others we think should meet those needs. When they don't meet our needs, conflict and stress develop.

Over time, and if these needs are not met, we may develop a sense of "learned helplessness." We learn we are destined to the life we are currently living, and no matter how much we do or try, we always seem to be stuck and hurt. Each new day is a "copy" and "paste" from the one before. Ironically, these same emotions and experiences that make us feel stuck are the same emotions and experiences that could enable our growth, if we learn how to do so. This book will help you understand what drives you to think, feel, and behave the way you do, and it will help you more fully meet your needs and fulfill your potential.

I want to acknowledge that many of the ideas presented in this new framework are not completely new, and have been influenced by the works of Abraham Maslow, Erik Erikson, John Bowlby, Mary Ainsworth, and others. I am also indebted to the field of resiliency and its authors, especially Robert Brooks and Sam Goldstein. Whether repurposed, repackaged, recycled, or revised, the foremost purpose of this framework is to give a straightforward and practical method for helping individuals cope with loss. The reader or critic can decide for themselves if it constitutes a new theory or not.

More importantly, my appreciation is given to those who freely shared their thoughts and stories with me. Some of their names have been changed, and details from several of their stories have been omitted in order to protect their privacy, relationships, and lives. I have also drawn upon other sources as they become relevant to various "potential" themes.

NOTES

Achor, S. (2010). *The Happiness Advantage: The Seven Principles of Positive Psychology That Fuel Success and Performance at Work (2010).* USA: Crown Business.

Brooks, R., & Goldstein, S. (2004). *The Power of Resilience: Achieving Balance, Confidence, and Personal Strength in Your Life.* New York: McGraw-Hill (p. 31).

Goleman, D., (1995). *Emotional Intelligence.* New York, NY: Bantam Books, Inc. (p. 43).

Oher, M. (2012). *I Beat The Odds: From Homelessness, to The Blind Side, and Beyond.* New York: Penguin.

Section 2

Chapter 4: To Feel Safe Again

The first and most basic human need is Safety. Physiological needs, such as food, water, shelter, and clothing are the easiest to identify based on one's appearance or what a refrigerator or closet looks like. But even when those things are provided, victims of loss may still not feel safe.

Many who have experienced loss have been hurt by those who should have cared for them. The reality that someone (or worse, someone who "loved" you) hurt you increases the perception that you can be hurt again, and you might struggle with loving others because you are afraid to be hurt like that again. Hurt can be inflicted in a variety of ways, whether it be verbal, emotional/mental, physical, sexual, spiritual, or through neglect. It is also important to make sure that our perceptions of safety are accurate and healthy.

Safety needs are largely expected to be met in childhood by our parents. But when these needs go unmet, they become hardwired into a child's emotional DNA, and are invisible influences for how we see the world, even as adults.

One of my first interviewees, Liana Luna, experienced her mother and stepfather's divorce, and remembered feeling completely abandoned. In the years that followed, she sought people, experiences, and drugs to help her feel like she was re-connecting with her stepdad, and found herself homeless for many of those years. You may not have experienced homelessness, but you can likely relate with her plea of, "Why me?" If you frequently ask yourself,

"Why me?" you might also be struggling with meeting your safety need, and it's important to recognize how feeling unsafe, abandoned, or alone may serve as an unconscious drive toward people or situations that make you feel safe, even if the reality is that they may not be good for you.

Comparable feelings may exist among parents who observe a loss of, in, or with their children. When your child is hurt, you are likely to wonder, "Why didn't I protect my child?" or, "Can't I even keep my child safe?" Parents who experience child loss are more likely to talk about safety in terms of whether other members of their family are going to be safe, or they may have concerns that the victimized member of their family can become re-victimized.

Bryn Barton experienced this very thing. Bryn is a mother of two daughters, one of whom was kidnapped and sold into sex trafficking. This instilled in her a chronic fear that victimization could happen again. Shortly after my interview with Bryn, I met another parent, this time a father, whose daughter was also kidnapped, and finally returned after six days of not knowing where she was. Understandably, this father and Bryn were both very frustrated that the police did not respond quicker and more efficiently.

These parents' experiences made me wonder how often we are upset with those who, like the police, symbolize safety but are the targets of our frustration when we do not feel safe. When considering relationships, in general, it does seem to explain why we are often critical of the people we love when we don't feel safe, because we have equated "love" to feeling safe.

For many dealing with the death of a loved one, what hurts most is there are no do-overs. We cannot go back into the past and be a better parent, be more involved, be a better child, more kind, more anything. Even our language suggests a distancing between us and our loved ones. "My child *was* smart. My child *was* a great athlete. My parent *was* the only one who was kind to me. My child *was* funny. My mother *was* beautiful."

Unsafe Triggers

In these kinds of experiences, as well as with many other kinds or types of loss experiences, logic flies out the window and our behaviors are driven by emotion. We may buy things or "buy into" philosophies that aren't good for us, whether it's the latest supplement, drug, hobby, or relationship. Just as the most desperate person is likely to get swindled in a car deal, we keep going back to things that aren't good for our emotional, financial, and sometimes physical well-being.

When we feel unsafe, it isn't uncommon to be "set off" or experience "triggers" from certain people or events, leading to a sense of rage, despair, or hopelessness. Recognizing what those triggers are is only the first step, and trying to step outside one's own perception is the next step, calming or quieting the hurt from the past.

These triggers, thoughts, and emotions often make a person feel different, or more precisely, detached, from other people and their experiences. As noted by Laurence

Gonzales, author of *Surviving survival: The art and science of resilience*, "feelings of alienation and displacement represent one of the most common responses to trauma" (p. 4). Being isolated from others further fuels fears of not being safe, because now we don't know if others are "with us" or not. This sense of not knowing if we belong, either in a family or with our friends, is what Pauline Boss refers to as "ambiguous loss."

Several of the individuals I interviewed talked about how these triggers push the body and mind into high alert and suspicion. For example, if someone hurt your child or hurt you, when you meet someone who reminds you of that person, it brings back those feelings and memories. Even TV shows, movies, and observing others can create sudden fears or resentment, often accompanied with the original memory of your loss. Sometimes confusion can result from these experiences as well.

For some individuals, their experience with a loss of safety is felt most when they don't get enough "quiet time." These individuals may feel "jumpy," finding the close of a door or click of a light switch troublesome to their sense of sanity and peace. Each event or episode seems to trigger a sense of fear, panic, or desperation. The more they try to convince themselves they are safe, the more they seem to find reasons to not feel safe.

Sometimes our triggers occur when others are celebrating an event we feel robbed of, when others try to convince us that everything is okay, or make us feel that we are not the ones experiencing the loss.

Carrie and Jared, married parents of two children, were expecting their third child when they discovered Carrie had a molar pregnancy. A molar pregnancy consists of tissue that, instead of forming a baby, becomes an abnormal growth in the uterus. For some time, Carrie continued to visit the clinic for health care, but found it difficult to go there because of the emotional pain she experienced while listening to others who were preparing for the delivery of their child. Some people told her, "Well, at least you already have two children," trying to comfort her. But couldn't she find joy in her children while feeling pain from her loss?

The reality is we seldom make the connection between difficult emotions and the true impact they have on us and our relationships. Instead, we wonder, "Why am I feeling like that? What is my problem? Why can't I get over it?"

Not feeling safe makes us even more suspicious of other people's motives and behavior, and not having the "safety" need met heightens our sensitivities for how people treat us. And it influences how we respond to them and how they treat us. For example, when having a disagreement with a spouse or co-worker, being suspicious of their actions or intent translates into nonverbal cues to the other person that you don't like them, trust them, or believe them. This will likely lead them to feel the same way about you.

Changing Our Thoughts About The Lack of Safety

It takes a great deal of effort to change our thought processes when we do not feel safe around others. This is because our brains are already wired to perceive things and people a certain way based on our earlier experiences. Like a river that flows along the path of least resistance, we continue to think the same way we've been programmed. Our brains are built for efficiency and survival, not reality; habits are formed, and our brains (and emotions) are designed to feel as minimally taxed as possible (although some days you may not believe it) as well as survival. This state of cognitive efficiency, simplicity, and survival works well for much of the time, but when we find ourselves in a continual cycle of fear and unsafe relationships, changing how we think is just as important as changing what we think.

To Fear or Not to Fear

Conduct an Internet search for inspirational quotes about combating fear, and you'll find thousands of words or phrases people have used to cope with fear. Some of those quotes are useful in some contexts while ineffective in others.

One of my favorite quotes about fear is by Franklin Roosevelt, who said, "The only thing we have to fear is fear itself." An adult child who realizes his imagination is scarier than confronting his parents may find the courage to confront that fear and tell himself, and perhaps his parents, that he is not to blame for their choices.

One of the temptations during (and after) loss is to suppress our fears or pain. While we need to learn how to manage those emotions and hurts, continually pushing them aside eventually builds up, and it's best to vent as safely and quickly as possible. As Bryn Barton, a mother of a daughter kidnapped and sold into human trafficking, said, "Don't be afraid to feel. You have to, or else you'll explode."

One person who faced this fear and conquered it was Stephanie Nielson, a popular "mommy blogger" who experienced a horrendous plane crash, burning much of her body. After being in a coma for several months, she woke up in a body she did not recognize. I remember watching one of the videos with Stephanie speaking, where she talked about her early struggles of not wanting her children to see her the way she was, of the pain when her children would see her but look away, and of her knowledge that others were filling her "mommy" role. Her very sense of self was questioned. Stephanie is an inspiration to me and others because she confronted her fear by committing to get her family back, to be their mom, no matter what.

However, fear isn't always a bad thing to have. It may be useful at times. If you grew up with manipulative parents, your fear of manipulation may dissuade you from forming a relationship with someone who may want to manipulate you. Or if a child becomes seriously injured due to drinking and driving, it's reasonable for a parent to be concerned when they see or hear about another one of their children drinking alcohol.

And so it is a balance: Allowing fear to motivate you to be safe but not allowing it to crush your resolve. There is a difference between having a bird's eye view and a worm's eye view. Knowing what is "out there" is good, but focusing on everything and anything that can eat at you is very much a problem. Not every Greek gift carries a Trojan horse. Keeping the right perspective about fear is incredibly important for maintaining our sanity.

Another, albeit silly, analogy for fear was given to me from my teen son, who I found outside one day jumping off our roof and onto our trampoline. Fear instinctively coursed through my body, and I rushed outside to question his sanity. "But Dad," he replied, "how can you know it's dangerous if you've never tried it?" The proper response should have been, "I've never tried lighting myself with kerosene oil, but I can still be confident it's dangerous."

Unfortunately, emotions took over and I was going to prove to him, once and for all, it was dangerous. When I climbed on top of the house, I realized that looking down (from on top the house to the trampoline) looked much further than looking up (from the trampoline to the roof). On top the roof, my knees buckled, my palms were sweating, and I thought I was going to pass out. But my ego was strong, and stupid, and I jumped. Actually, because of my fear, I fell rather than jumped, and nearly missed the trampoline located directly under our roof. Facing my fear (albeit reluctantly) nearly got me killed, and it increased my fear of heights even more.

For Tabatha, a young adult college student struggling with learning disabilities and other losses, the way she is able to visualize and then let go of unneeded stress and fear is by writing down what she feels, and then she puts it through a paper shredder. "There is more to life than just stressing out over silly things," she reminds herself.

Rebecca Mahan, a police officer and author of *V.O.T.E.,* which stands for Victims Overcoming Traumatic Events, teaches others that one of the first steps for moving past their sense or experience of loss is to identify why they are afraid and what the source of that fear is. As noted by Mahan, there are many sources or reasons for fear, including being afraid of God's displeasure, fear for another person's well-being, and fear of not being loved or of value.

It would be good for each of us to remind ourselves there's more to life than stressing over silly things, even if it isn't always an easy thing to do. Each day at work, I take an elevator up to the third floor to my office, and inside the elevator, a small piece of paper is taped above the panel. It reads: "In case of emergency, do not panic." It's very difficult not to panic when we feel we are in danger. Our brains are wired to survive, and especially following trauma, we are often hyper vigilant to other things, events, and people whom we think will be traumatic for us. Our oversensitivity is much like breaking the glass of the fire extinguisher casing when someone lights a birthday candle.

The reason for this hypersensitivity is natural, but it isn't healthy. Our bodies, like our minds, store memories and are ready to protect us from any future danger—even perceived danger.

In reality, our bodies have minds of their own, as evidenced by the times you get sick to your stomach from nerves, or tense up around a person, but aren't sure why. If we gave conscious thought to every single stress, our minds would be overloaded; our minds are simply seeking to be as efficient as possible.

I once read a study showing that, years after Mt. St. Helen's had erupted on May 18, 1980, the communities surrounding the mountain had experienced a major increase in the number of health problems. Some surmised it must be because of the content from the ash spewed, which cannot be underestimated. I was 9-years-old at the time, living in eastern Washington, and I walked out of church with small flakes of ash falling down on me. Within just minutes, visibility had gone from 100 percent to zero, and each night and snowstorm following were reminders of the reality of that day and the fear many experienced because of it.

The incidences of disease and mood challenges have been shown to escalate following trauma, whether it's a volcanic eruption or failure to get a job after months of trying. All of these things suggest that our need to be safe goes far beyond one event, and extends into the days and years following the traumatic event.

Research has also shown that those who are married to a critical spouse are much more likely to develop a disease than those who do not live with a critical spouse, and chances are that these kinds of experiences can reduce your feelings of safety, leading to a shutdown of your body. Whether the impact of these traumatic experiences are directly impacting one's physical functions, the emotional and mental impact of such experiences can literally make you sick. Some simply choose not to feel, hoping to protect themselves from its effects. But like the person who never pays attention to their car alarm going off in the middle of the night, left unchecked, those somatic, or psychosomatic, experiences could lead to considerable problems later on.

Challenges with the safety need are almost always preceded by thoughts of scarcity. "I'm not enough. They can't love me—that much. There's not enough of me to do everything. I'm not smart enough. They might accept me now, but would they if they knew who I really was?" It's looking at the paycheck, and instead of seeing the numbers coming into your life and wallet, you see it being siphoned away quicker than it came. With that perspective, it's easy to get jealous of others when they have good luck or good experiences, and to be fearful that they are taking what you want or need for yourself.

Our thoughts often are given voice, according to Michael Singer, author of *The Untethered Soul: The Journey Beyond Yourself*, by a psychotic-like narrator. The advice Singer gives is to imagine that the voice in your head actually has a body, and is always talking to you. "Why did you do that? Why did you do it like that?" Even when you try to sit down and watch your favorite show, that psychotic-like inner person won't let you be. Singer recommends that we imagine our thoughts having a body of their own, and to imagine that person following you, making you crazy, trying to take control of everything you want to do. That voice is not you, but rather a psychotic narrator of events and experiences that sometimes needs to shut up. It is an echo of words, experiences, and interpretations from your past experiences and relationships. It is not you.

Sometimes changing the imagery can also be an effective method for overcoming negative self-talk. Some methods may require a skilled professional. Consider the following words and practice of Chris Delaney, a hypnotherapist and NLP Life Coach.

> *I teach the client to turn the voice into a shape and then to imagine this shape moving down their body. As the shape moves down the body, the power of the negative self-talk vanishes. I encourage practice, as repetition is the key to learning a new skill and as you practice feeling different to the same situation the neurons create new pathways, new way of unconscious responses.*

A victim and survivor are both likely to struggle with these voices, largely formed to make sense of what they had gone through. "Making sense" is, unfortunately, not the same thing as being factual or even helpful. This is the same voice that tells you to feel guilty about everything you do, and when you commit to not feeling guilty, it gets aggressive. *You should have been a better girl and your parents would have loved you. Do you remember that one time, when you did that one thing? Fine, don't feel guilty, but that's just cold. That's not very (fill in the blank) of you. If you haven't forgiven that person yet, perhaps the problem really was you. What would others think of you if they only knew the whole story?*

Again, treat the inner voice or your thoughts just as you would someone else telling you these things. Those words are uncalled for. At some point, realizing those inner thoughts are broken reflections, and not a true image of who you really are, is the key to ignoring them.

Many times, the voices in our heads make us feel guilty and ashamed. Brene' Brown, author of several books addressing vulnerabilities, clarifies that there is a difference between guilt and shame, but notes that many of us struggle with recognizing that difference. Brown suggests that guilt is something that says, "What you've done is wrong," and shame means "Who you are is wrong." Learn to recognize when you feel each; sometimes guilt can help you learn to repair harm, but shame has little to no value.

One technique for learning how to change your thoughts, which will often change your feelings of doubt or insecurity, is called "reframing." This strategy is the human equivalent to editing digital pictures, where you choose what to focus your attention on. Just as computers can "touch up" pictures, or frame a portion of a picture at the exclusion of the rest, humans are capable of narrowing or widening our focus to make sure the memory or thought looks or works good. It's a technique I encouraged quite heavily in one of my earlier books, but my perception of this strategy took a new direction when I read the book *David and Goliath*, by Malcolm Gladwell, who described England's response to being bombed by the Germans during World War I in terms of "hits" and "near misses." According to Gladwell, many of England's residents believed that escaping from the bombing raids made them invincible, and in turn, created the courage that Germans had thought would instead be fear and despair. Changing our perception of our experiences, realizing we are still here, breathing, functioning, and leading lives that require something of us will help us change our fear into courage.

The Target Always Changes and is Never Good Enough

Being shamed by those you love or who (should) love you is particularly hurtful. It often leads to withdrawing from that person in order to avoid feeling hurt or pain. Being shamed by others is hurtful, in part, because it is personal. Here is the person you love, trust, and depend on, and they are telling you that you are not enough (or good enough) for them.

Those who struggle with feeling safe likely feel that the target for what they are supposed to be or do constantly changes, and that the expectations are unrealistic. First, you have to work more, now you need to work less, but still you need to make more money. You need to be more assertive then you're criticized when you're more assertive. You need to spend more time with the children then you are not parenting the "right way." When you become the child, parent, or spouse they say they want, you discover it's what they wanted yesterday, not today. On the highway of life where the street signs and rules of the road change each minute, it's easy to lose a sense of security and gain a sense of distrust for others.

What is the difference between complaining, criticism, and shaming? Complaining means you're not happy with the way things are, criticism says you're not happy with what that person is, and shaming is personal attack intended to devalue another. In my opinion, one way to recognize whether a person is complaining about you, criticizing you, or shaming you is by how you feel. Complaining often makes a person feel frustrated, criticism makes a person feel defensive, and shaming leads to a loss of hope and value.

To Trust Again

Most people who experience a major loss, and particularly those who aren't supported in that loss, experience an additional loss-- a loss of trust. Dr. Samantha Madhosingh, a psychologist and life coach, explains it this way:

Trust is the biggest thing that gets derailed from loss. Trust has been violated. Regaining trust and feeling that safety and security is very important to have. I don't think you can have hope without trust. Trust is critical to the resiliency process, to bounce back.

Similarly, Arlinda D. Lindsay, LCSW, LCAC, who provides therapy for individuals who were sexually abused as children and are struggling with those emotions as adults, says, "First and foremost, they have to feel safe, to trust again…before they can learn of their value." And Patrick Manis, human behavior expert and celebrity life coach, explained that a person who feels safe will be more likely to trust others.

> *My definition of trust is safety. I feel safe with you. If I say I feel safe with you, it means you either accept me, you approve of me, you're going to follow through with what you said you'd do, and you're going to show up at the time you said you'd show up. What's beneath trust is safety.*

Not only are loss victims and survivors having difficulty trusting others, many "believers" find it difficult to trust their God or a higher power after experiencing loss. Some find that their faith crumbles as a result of that loss and sense of distrust, while others find their faith is what helps them eventually learn to trust again and live a satisfying life. Some experience both. Lisa Ford-Berry, the mother of Michael, a teen who was bullied and committed suicide, said it this way.

> *Not only was I in physical pain, but the first time in my life, my faith didn't help. I had a crisis in faith. I had been faithful. And I thought, Why me? We did everything we were supposed to. I didn't cut corners. And to have something like this happen seemed so unfair. It took years, but I made it through faith, a promise, that whatever doors open, I'll serve wherever called. Life is much richer now.*

Distrusting God, or at least feeling betrayed by God or a Higher Power, is a common theme for many experiencing the painful effects of loss. *I trusted Him. Why would God do this to me?*

From all the interviews I conducted, this issue of what or whom to trust was central to meeting their safety needs. Some reconnected their faith to God, gaining a sense of purpose from their trial, while others were more likely to gain greater trust in their family, themselves, science or philosophical views. For many, like Lisa, they experienced a seesaw battle between trust and mistrust, at least for some time. Of course, this doesn't mean we should trust everyone. For example, if someone abused you as a child, allowing them to babysit your children should be met with serious caution.

Jared and Carrie, the young married couple I mentioned earlier, also found trust to be a central issue in each of their experiences with loss. Sometime after they had a molar pregnancy, Carrie got pregnant again, and felt her pregnancy was a blessing or reward for having gone through her trial with the previous pregnancy. But joy turned to unbearable pain, and a child symbolizing God's trust in her was lost through a miscarriage. Her husband, Jared, tried to comfort Carrie, yet struggled with his own loss and emotions that came from it.

Jared grew up in a large family, and was often physically and emotionally abused as a child by his father. His dad told Jared and his siblings they would not become anything good in life and used sticks to spank them daily. When the sticks wore down, he started using a PCP pipe. "He found a solution that wasn't going to break," Jared explained. Shortly after graduating from high school, Jared knew he had to get out, moving from California to Idaho.

> *I tried to hold onto this hope that they would change, that I would go home, and we would work through it. But my dad called a few days before Christmas [while I was away] and disowned me. That was the nail in the coffin. It was hard to get through every single day. And I found out the things I had shared privately with my mom [about my dad's actions], those things she told my dad. I had always thought my mom was the victim in all of this, but I realized she played a part in it. I had been betrayed.*

Jared had also served in the military, and was deployed to Qatar and Iraq, where he provided security detail. Perceptions of danger escalated under a manipulative supervisor, who served as a trigger, a reminder of Jared's dad, and the abuse he suffered under his hand. "I learned I couldn't trust those in authority, so how could I feel safe when I could not trust?" he asked.

For both Jared and his wife, Carrie, their loss actually fueled their motivation to trust their faith even more. They looked to their God and faith for meaning, purpose, and motivation. "The only thing to help me when I had nothing left was putting all my faith and all my trust in God, and that built me into a totally new person," Jared recounted.

Whereas some people struggle with trusting those in authority, sometimes those in authority have a challenge with trusting those they lead. I find that this is especially true for parents who had previously experienced great loss in their lives; learning to trust your children, even adult children, is something some parents struggle with.

Chelsea, who has been a widow for decades, had an adult daughter who gave up her career ambitions to live off Chelsea's credit cards, racking up tens of thousands of dollars of debt. As a mother, Chelsea felt she had to rescue her daughter, despite her daughter's age and choices in life. After counseling, advice from her friend, and other experiences, Chelsea cut the purse strings, and started trusting that her daughter would learn from her choices. Trusting your children to make the right choices, and trusting that they will learn from their mistakes, are difficult lessons for many parents to learn.

I believe having this balance of trusting ourselves and trusting others is key to moving beyond being the victim and becoming a true survivor. Loral Lee Portenier, a transpersonal psychologist, and licensed clinical professional counselor, expresses the importance of trust in this way.

> *Trust the process. I like to place the focus on restoring personal power, especially when there's not a clear reason for the why of life circumstances. This helps to increase one's sense of resilience because if we know we have access to our own inner power and wisdom, we can bend with the winds, the storms of life, instead of breaking. By bending and surviving, we can learn to trust that we have the inner strength to not only heal from current or past trauma and loss, but from that which we have yet to encounter on our life path.*

A large percentage of people who experience loss attempt to go on with their lives without addressing the pain or loss of trust that came from that loss. To some degree, the reason why many of us do not work on trust issues is: (1) We are afraid to trust again, or (2) We do not think we have trust issues. It could be denial, but for most people it's simply a lack of evidence. We fall in love, form relationships, and life seems to be going along smoothly. There simply isn't the motivation to work on trust issues until they start to surface.

If you have experienced a significant loss and have not sought to confront the issues of distrust, pain, or abandonment from that loss, you will likely experience those emotions or thoughts when dealing with stress, conflict, or fear. You may even be overprotective of the ones you love, which can cause its own set of problems.

Chronic worrying is another sign your trust reservoirs have been depleted too often. Worrying isn't necessarily bad, but when it keeps you from living or enjoying life, it is excessive. Our brains have created excessive worrying as its own replacement for trust, because when we worry, bad things tend to not happen. We worry about what we see on TV happening to us, losing our jobs, or having our children kidnapped. Our brains make the connection of "I worry" and "it doesn't happen" so it becomes a magical replacement for trusting.

When my children were little, I occasionally drove down the road honking my horn. When they asked what I was doing, I said I was keeping the elephants off the road—in Sacramento, California. "No, you're not," they'd yell in unison. "Well," I replied, "Do you see any elephants?" If we are going to learn to trust again, we need to confront the fallacy that our worries are making us safe.

Another challenge with feeling safe and trusting others is when we are constantly in transition. Many foster children have had challenges trusting the process for this reason. Research has frequently shown that the more displacements a foster child experiences, the greater likelihood of them developing internal (e.g. depression) or external (e.g. aggression) problems. Of course, most youth in foster care programs do just fine, but the more changes they experience, the more difficult it is for them to know whom they can trust or rely on for their safety needs.

Frequent displacements, whether going through the foster system or from other life changes, may also serve as triggers for not feeling safe. Abrupt changes in a job, marital status, or social life may reduce your sense of security, even if those events are initially considered positive. The important thing to remember is that our bodies and minds view any kind of stress as stressful, whether it's negative (i.e. unwanted) or positive (i.e. wanted) stress; reducing the number of sudden transitions in our lives may help us feel safe and be more likely to trust ourselves and others around us.

Be pro-active for feeling safe; in most cases, you can do more about this than you imagine. Don't wait for someone else to help you feel safe; it often becomes a heavy burden for others to always prove that they can be trusted to help you feel safe. Create your own environment for learning to trust and feel safe again.

Types of Trust

Just as there are different forms of "loss," there are also different forms of trust. In their work on "trust building®" with people and organizations, Dr. Dennis Reina and Dr. Michelle Reina identify three Dimensions of Trust: The Three Cs®: (1) Trust of Character™, (2) Trust of Communication™, and (3) Trust of Capability™ and 16 specific behaviors that build trust. Trust of Character refers to trusting the other person that they'll do what they say they'll do, Trust of Communication refers to the openness and ability of being able to effectively talk and listen. Trust of Capability is built when two people learn to trust each other's abilities and talents.

Whether you're the person who needs to trust yourself again or the one who is trying to rebuild their trust with another, these three Dimensions of Trust can be helpful for understanding what you or another person specifically need. *When I say I need to trust you, I mean I need to trust that you will pick up the kids when you say you will (Trust of Character). I appreciate all the hard work you are doing to help me, but what I really need is the talking, listening, and discussing —that would help me feel safe again (Trust of Communication). When you say you want to trust me again, do you mean you need me to improve on a particular skill (Trust of Capability), talk or listen more (Trust of Communication), or that you feel I'm not doing what I say I would do for you as a spouse/friend/sibling/parent (Trust of Character)?*

In their book *Trust and Betrayal in the Workplace: Building Effective Relationships in Your Organization,* the authors point out that positive acknowledgement from others builds and strengthens our trust in ourselves and in others. The analogy of a developing child is used to illustrate the evolution of trust, as a positive parental response to attempts at crawling, walking, and talking will elicit and increase the trust that the child has in his parents to take even more risks, believing that the end result will be a successful and pleasing one. Emotionally, you may need to learn to walk, or even crawl again, before you can run. Surround yourself with those who are supportive in your attempt to trust again, and limit the influences of those who try to convince you that you can no longer trust (yourself or others) again. When you do this, you will feel greater confidence in yourself and seek to take even greater risks to strengthen your sense of self-trust and trust in others. [1]

Safety and Trust Antagonists

Negative emotions, particularly those focusing inward (meaning toward ourselves), make us feel unsafe. As both an ancient and revived emphasis for dealing with physiological responses from shame, useless guilt, and internal criticism, breathing exercises may provide some relaxation and confidence building. There are hundreds of different types of breathing exercises; whichever you try, it's usually best to have an environment that is quiet and limits distraction. One method is to lie down on your back, close your eyes, and count to 60, with each combination of inhalation and exhalation being one count. Do your best to focus on the breath and nothing else. If you feel particularly stressed, count to 100. Count slowly, but breathe comfortably. If you become distracted or even angry while breathing, tell yourself what you are feeling, and learn to be okay with it. I find that ear buds, noise cancellation headphones, or if necessary, substituting lying down with a quiet walk through nature, can be quite relaxing. There are people who feel most relaxed while smelling pleasant scents, such as those found in some essential oils. Some individuals like to breathe softly so they can't even hear their breathing, and others like to breathe loudly. Experiment with each to see which style you like best.

---

[1] These terms are registered trademarks of Reina Trust Building Institute, LLC (1995-2015).

Either way, focus on your breath, and try to ignore everything else that annoying voice in your mind is telling you to do. Focus is an emotional muscle, and it will take time to master.

Focus can be developed in some of our most menial tasks. If you are especially stressed, you may find yourself eating food quicker than you should. Stress increases feelings of scarcity, and scarcity is a trigger that increases our drive to get whatever we can, as quickly as we can. Most people can relate to watching a suspenseful, action-packed, or scary movie while eating a big bag of popcorn or chips and wondering where all the food went. If you find yourself consistently eating your food too quickly because of stress, learning to force yourself to eat slowly, meaning to chew your food slowly, is a conscious approach to relaxing your body and mind.

Dr. Lisa Bahar, a marriage and family therapist and drug and alcohol counselor, recommends practices to help with "self-soothing" and a form of self-soothing known as distraction. Self-soothing is about consciously looking for things or experiences to help reduce your feelings of stress, perhaps while dealing with the stressful event, while distraction is placing a greater focus on something so you won't have to immediately deal with the very thing that is taxing your emotions and health.

> *Self-soothing is being able to create an environment to feel safe and comforted. It may be a warm, fuzzy blanket or slippers or flannel sheets representing touch and warmth or something that is more visually appealing like a bouquet of flowers or*

*candle that represent a kinder, gentler kind of
mood. The goal is create a calming environment,
lighting a fire, peaceful music, or having your dog
nearby. Distraction can be a help or hindrance; it is
a skill and it takes practice. Distraction is used to
stabilize the emotions and mind, and they're there
to deal with a problem you can't solve and you just
can't afford to make it worse.—Dr. Bahar*

Take at least some time each day, separated from others,
with all forms of technology turned off, to practice being
free from outside stressors. This doesn't mean we will be
completely free from our own thoughts, but we will be free
from having to worry about the next email, phone call, or
text; this will allow us to focus on controlling our own
thoughts through breathing exercises or meditation. Or it
may be realizing those worries are there, but giving oneself
the freedom from having to do anything about them right
then.

Of course, it's much easier to focus on our breathing when
our bodies are working correctly. Unfortunately, when we
experience pain, loss, and many forms of stress, our bodies
are often the first thing to "go." Either we eat too much, too
little, or not the right foods. One of the symptoms for not
feeling safe can be anxiety, which Trudy Scott, a food
mood expert and author of *The Anti-Inflammatory Food
Solution*, notes can either be a cause of nutritional
deficiencies, especially with zinc and B6, or a condition
known as pyroluria.

According to Scott, proteins, notably GABA and
Tryptophan, and evening primrose oil may be helpful for

dealing with anxiety. Our stress levels skyrocket when we lose sleep, forget to exercise, or when we exercise *too much*, leading to long-term exhaustion. Remember to create healthy boundaries between those things stealing your energy and your ability to make decisions, even if you feel like you "just have to do it." For example, having a goal of running a mile each day is a good goal, but if it makes you more tired than energized in the long-term, it's time to cut back.

While moments of quiet are essential, there are times music may also help calm the body and mind. Be careful when over-stimulating your senses with loud or fast-paced music. Although you may initially feel more energetic with upbeat music, playing peaceful music will likely benefit you more in the long run if your body and mind need to be in a calm state.

Recharging the Batteries for Introverts

We can get lost in various social experiments, trying to escape our pain. Parties, social networking, and continual texting often make us feel busy and connected with others. Although it's good to reach out and form friendships with others, the goal during this time for resolving pain and loss should be finding what works best for you. Ask yourself, "Are they effective?"

In her groundbreaking book, *Quiet*, author Susan Cain emphasizes the different ways individuals respond to stress. Some people have their emotional and mental batteries charged by being around people, whereas for others, it is exhausting. Keep a journal for how you feel before, during, and after those experiences to determine if you need to make some social adjustments to increase your energy. Ask your friends and family members for help, and let them know it's for your health.

If Safety is Unlikely

Thus far, the focus has been on how to resolve not feeling safe. Many times by increasing our emotional capacity to feel safe and to trust again, we actually change our circumstances and future experiences that lead us to feeling safer and more trusting of others. But there may be times when physical or emotional safety may not feel completely possible. Here are three steps to increase your own potential and of those around you:

#1. Recognize how your insecure feelings impact those you care about.

#2. Acknowledge those feelings to yourself and to those most impacted. "Owning" the fear, or taking responsibility for it, is courageous. Courageous people do great things by facing their fears.

#3. Develop strategies (in advance) for what to do when you don't feel safe, so that you do not "take it out" on those who are dependent on you. Examples may include therapy, books, journaling, and other hobbies fostering stress-free creativity.

Medical help may also be necessary. For example, cortisol is a hormone controlled by the adrenal gland, which is the "fight or flight" response to fear and stress. It's the "can do" hormone. Having chronically low levels may make you feel lethargic and unconfident, and may require some supplementation, while chronically high levels lead to anxiety and a deterioration of muscle and bone structure.

The thyroid gland, also responsible for several hormones, and a potential cause of anxiety, has also received a great deal of attention over the last few years, and there may be medical or alternative approaches for improving the thyroid and/or adrenal glands that work well for you. If possible, avoid the "try everything right now" approach, taking it one step at a time.

Boundaries are also very important during this time. You may need to set a limit for how much time you spend with those who make you feel unsafe; you may also want to commit to a specific amount of time per day or week to be with people who help you feel safe. In my previous book, *Grow Your Marriage by Leaps & Boundaries,* I defined boundaries as lines we draw to protect or prioritize things, people, and relationships. The boundary you may need to draw is one that prioritizes your health over having a perfectly clean house. Or you may need to tell your spouse you need one evening per week to spend by yourself engaged in a new hobby. You might also need to tell your children you need to go to bed by 9 pm until you are no longer sleep deprived. Or it may be that anytime you catch yourself feeling sorry for yourself, you commit to helping another person. The goal is to limit the negativity and stress in your life until your nerves and spirit feel strong enough to battle those things again.

Some fears are so hard-wired they require expert assistance. Allow yourself the option of seeking proper counseling or treatment, for your own health's sake and for those you love. If you are looking for therapeutic options, do as much research as possible, and ask specifically what kind of work that counselor or organization has done with traumatized individuals and families. Ask if, and where, they received their training.

It's not uncommon for those suffering from trauma to be diagnosed with Post-Traumatic Stress Disorder (PTSD), which is where recurring events trigger emotions and memories from that original trauma, leading one to repeat (i.e. recycle) their exposure to intense stress and pain over and over again.

The first major clinical work for patients with PTSD was with soldiers who had come home from their tours of duty, and who struggled with re-assimilating into the "normal" world. Then, many professionals saw similar symptoms or characteristics of unhealthy responses in the general population; although they had not dealt with war, they had gone through their own emotional battlefield.

NOTES

Boss, P. (2002). *Family Stress Management (2nd Ed.).*
Thousand Oaks, CA: Sage.

Cook, J. (2012). *Grow Your Marriage by Leaps and Boundaries.* Cedar Fort: Utah.

Gladwell, M. (2013). *David and Goliath: Underdogs, Misfits, and the Art of Battling Giants.* New York: Little, Brown and Company.

Laurence Gonzales (2012). *Surviving survival: The art and science of resilience.* New York: W. W. Norton & Company.

Reina, D. & Reina, M. (2007). Building sustainable trust. *OD Practitioner, 39 (1)*, 36-41.
http://www.reinatrustbuilding.com/reinatrustbuilding.com/userfiles/file/ODN%20Building%20Sustainable%20Trust.pdf

Singer, M. (2007). *The Untethered Soul: The Journey Beyond Yourself.* Oakland, CA: New Harbinger Publications.

Stephanie Neilson blog.
http://nieniedialogues.blogspot.com/

Reina, D. & Reina, M. (2006). *Trust and Betrayal in the Workplace: Building Effective Relationships in Your Organization.* Berret Koehler: USA.

Scott, T. (2011). *The Antianxiety Food Solution: How the Foods You Eat Can Help You Calm Your Anxious Mind,*

Improve Your Mood, and End Cravings. Oakland, CA: New Harbinger Publications.

Susan Cain (2013). *Quiet: The Power of Introverts in a World That Can't Stop Talking.* New York: Broadway Books.

Chapter 5: Influence

At the earliest stages of life, humans desperately want to influence things and people. Infants cry, and if someone responds, they learn they have some influence over their surroundings or environment. The use of mobiles in cribs is another example. As soon as they are able, infants will touch, push, and kick the mobile in the crib, and they will do it repeatedly, to reaffirm they have some level of control (i.e. influence) over their surroundings. Or consider when an infant is in a high chair, and drops something, with you picking it up. That image or experience is so cool and rewarding to them that they will do it over and over again (while laughing at *your* silliness).

How strong is our need to influence others? Within the "Attachment" theory perspective, there are several observations where infants in orphanages were fed and clothed, but still died. The oft cited conclusion of these horrific experiences was that infants need physical affection to feel emotionally safe. But I believe it goes even deeper than that. Didn't the infants cry, initially, when they craved this affection? Won't infants stop crying when they realize no one will respond to their cries? The answer to each is "yes," and it showcases how instinctual (and fragile) our need is to influence others in a way that they respond in a positive way to us.

As adults, we may still have many of the needs we had as children or even as infants, and many therapeutic professionals work with the "inner child," tapping into the emotions and thoughts of the victim when the adult was a child to help address their needs. According to Rochelle Cook, an expert in clinical hypnotherapy and spiritual psychology, "The child self is going to be afraid and wonder why they were hurt and not protected. The inner child needs to be heard. One reason why is because a lot of these victims, when they do share [their emotions or experiences], have felt threatened, and when they talk about it [in a safe environment], there's a lot of healing right there."

Parenting

Fortunately, child raising practices have become more sensitive to the need for children to influence others, and parents are more likely today (compared to previous generations) to hold and hug children when they cry. Unfortunately, as children get older, many start to lose that sense of influence. They go to school, and now they have to raise their hands. Even if they raise their hands, they may not be selected. And if they are selected, they learn it's important to have the right answer, or at least the answer the teacher says is the right answer. Our sense of influence becomes increasingly dependent on whether our voices fit within a particular box, mold, or image.

Of course, rules and structure are very important, and we want to make certain we do not raise manipulative children. But when the pendulum shifts too far in the other direction, where they feel helpless or uncertain in sharing their voice or influence, that's when we stifle a child's potential.

As one of the most heralded authors on child abuse, Dave Pelzer experienced some of the worst cases of child abuse ever reported. His alcoholic mother called him "It," rather than by his real name, and beat him, sometimes resulting in broken bones. He was not allowed to speak until he was granted permission; he even needed permission to use the bathroom. A person who does not feel safe physically or emotionally is not likely to feel comfortable sharing their voice or influence. Their voice and influence, and even their sense of identity, are muted by events, perceptions, and people who should have kept them safe.

Wanting to Influence, Yet Feeling Restricted

When I first started my research for this book, many people came forward, initially willing to tell their story. However, it wasn't uncommon for some of those individuals to get "cold feet," which meant avoiding my follow-up contacts or, as the interview deadline got closer, start feeling sick to their stomachs. In a way, these individuals are also examples of the Potential Framework because the thought of sharing their stories (i.e. Influence) didn't make them feel safe; they had to feel safe *before* they felt comfortable sharing their story and influence. My hope is that I was effective at letting them know I understood their reasons for not participating, as relationships and lives are fragile, and their health and safety are of great importance.

I also hope those individuals who did not feel comfortable sharing their stories with me have at least one person to talk with about their stories. Having our voices and words matter are central to building our potential.

Imagine a child who comes inside the house and, finding their parent on the phone, talks incessantly to the parent, angering the parent. "I need you to be quiet," the parent may say. But that only seems to fuel the child's back-talking, temper tantrums, or taking it out on other siblings. The parent, recognizing the stern approach isn't working, and a little exhausted, may finally give in. "Hi Honey. Did you want to say something?" The child now looks relieved, nods "no," and goes back outside to play. The child has a simple but powerful need to be recognized and heard, or in other words, to have Influence. We all do.

One of the most common methods in therapy, and one way to give loss victims and survivors their sense of voice and influence, involves the Empty Chair. This is where the therapist places an empty chair in the room and asks the client to envision the person who harmed them sitting there, and the therapist is there to validate their emotions and help them heal from the trauma they experienced. "What do you want to tell (the perpetrator)?" the therapist might ask. The client will hopefully find a way to confront what they had seen as hanging over them and their life, with the hope of letting go in order to move on with their life. Although individuals can certainly conduct this experiment by themselves, or without a therapist, I do think it's best to use the empty chair in the presence of a trained professional; they can help buffer the negative emotions while helping you feel safe enough to express your pain.

There are literally countless examples of stories and studies finding that children who grow up in homes filled with criticism, violence, or uncertainty are most likely to develop emotional and behavioral problems. Let's consider just one study, published in the *Journal of Child Psychology and Psychiatry*, where the authors looked at the effects of children being bullied in elementary school. The authors found that children growing up in "low warmth" homes were more likely to exhibit emotional and behavioral problems as a result from being bullied, such as being more aggressive toward others. However, bullied children in high warmth homes tend to be buffered against the effects of bullying. The relevant aspect here is why is "warmth" so important? The answer is that it provides safety and trust, and that those who have difficulty developing those traits are more likely to use their influence in ways that hurt other people.

Recognizing the need for Influence in others may be one of the most difficult levels to assess. Chances are there have been times when your child shouted, "You never listen to me!" In most parent-child relationships the word "never" is a gross exaggeration. Most likely, there is a need within your child to be able to voice what they feel is important. Whereas some children feel comfortable speaking up, other children hold it inside until it either eats away at them or it explodes.

I'm not advocating that children go around telling off their parents, but I am advocating for a new perspective for many of us when working with children. When you are listening to your child, ask yourself, "Is this what my child really wants to share with me?" We can also reconnect with the earlier level or need by asking ourselves, "Does my child feel safe sharing what they feel is important to share?"

Not only do children seek to have an influence on their parents, parents also feel that they must have a positive influence on their children. This is obviously more difficult than it sounds, and the challenges of being influential for our children don't stop as they get older. One of the emotions that individuals, and particularly parents, feel when they don't have an adequate influence is that of *helplessness*. Consider the words of Judi, whose daughter ran away.

> *We want to be able to tell our children, "It's time to come home," and they reply, "Yes, mommy." But when that doesn't happen and you have no way of making it happen, you do feel helpless and not very influential. She wouldn't answer my calls; I really did feel helpless. She didn't care what I wanted. I had no influence. She was going to do what she wanted to do. Looking back, though, I'm kind of grateful for my daughter's ability to explore and take risks. It's worked out well for her."*

Judi's experience is a good example of recognizing that we do not need to influence all people, or even just those we love or feel responsible for, all the time. The important thing when we don't feel a sense of Influence is to come away from it with a positive message, value, or principle. For Judi, it was a sense of gratitude and being able to see risk taking as a positive trait that her daughter developed.

Singing

Have you ever sung in the shower, only to stop singing once you got out? The splashing of water from the showerhead has little to do with influence, but the privacy of being by ourselves makes us feel safe and confident to share our voice. Once we get out of the shower, we are more cognizant of how others may perceive our singing. (Or perhaps you enjoy whistling, but stop when others are watching).

Years ago, a woman talked about the importance of singing, and argued that church meetings would be much better if everyone sang loud and proud. At the end of her speech, she admitted her voice was not very good. I thought she was just being humble. But then in the process of proving her point, she sang a song a cappella. I thought, "I'm literally going to die. That is so awful!" Looking around the congregation, you could see the hair-raising response, like a teacher had just scratched her fingernails on the chalkboard. If that's what the heavenly choirs sounded like, I could see many asking for a demotion. Quickly, however, my look of shock turned to admiration as she proved we don't have to be perfect to share our voices. Or as my brothers often claim, "I don't sing well, but at least I sing loud."

Sharing Your Voice in Creative Ways

For those who struggle with talking about their loss, finding a creative outlet for sharing their talents and voice is essential. After the death of a loved one, some surviving family members have etched their loved one's names in stone, created a special kind of jewelry, or have named their backyard after their loved one. Some have created "chat" sessions online so that others who have experienced loss can have a means of sharing their thoughts and feelings without ridicule or embarrassment. One widow found comfort, a sense of community, and even humor while celebrating her husband's life during the anniversary of his death by interacting via social networking, asking her friends questions they can all answer: "What would you tell him if you saw him today? What was the craziest time you had with him? What do you miss most about him?" The most important thing is to make sure the feelings associated with loss do not bottle up. If you are looking to be supportive of someone who has experienced loss, support them in their creative (and yes, sometimes even bizarre) choices as much as possible. "Getting over" their loss isn't as healthy as making sense of it all.

In preparing for this book, I asked several individuals the following question: "How do you creatively honor your own loss or the loss of a loved one?" I literally received so many emailed responses I could not keep up with them. A large percentage of the emails involved honoring the death of a loved one by making certain that their loved one's voice and dreams stayed alive. One man said his father wanted to be an organ donor but could not because of his cancer-ridden body, so after the death of the father, the rest of the family signed up to be organ donors. Another example includes remembering the life and the death of a mother with the surviving daughters shopping on their mother's death anniversary; they buy something they absolutely don't need because they recall their mom's words, "Just get that."

For those who have had loved ones pass away, these simple acts of being able to recall the *life* during the anniversaries of death are excellent ways for connecting your voice and influence to those you have lost. Below is only one of the many emails I received about how to honor the loss experience of someone you care about:

> *I saw your question and couldn't believe that someone would be interested in knowing what I did to honor the anniversary of my dad's death. My father passed away when I was twelve years old. This past February was 25 years since his death. I decided that his memory, which should be a blessing, should be recognized in my social network in a public forum.*
>
> *In January, I reached out to family and friends for old photos of my dad. I requested funny stories, quips, and entertaining memories. People gladly shared. Every day this past February, I posted on my Facebook wall a photo and/or a memory of my dad in celebration of who he was. He never saw me graduate high school or college. He never saw me fall in love. Or get married. Or buy a house. Or have children. Or run a successful business. But that doesn't mean I'll forget who he was to me as an integral and critical life-shaper in my universe for twelve years.*
>
> *In a very global social media style, I posted this personal collection of pictures and memories to my 1,000+ friends on Facebook. I shared on Twitter. And maybe once related it to business and put it on LinkedIn. My family loved it. They in turn re-shared and retweeted the stories and images. More people got to "know" and talk about my amazing Dad. ALL*

MONTH LONG. It was cathartic. And amazing.
And a little weird to honor the death date of
someone. But, I looked past the oddness and boldly
did it. The feedback was sensational. Normally, I go
about my mundane suburban life of work and family
and might not think about my father daily. But not
this February. His memory burned brightly and I
felt great. Thank you for letting me share.--- Dana
Marlowe

"I'm There For You"

We can help loss victims and survivors strengthen their
sense of Influence by letting them share their stories with
us, and explain how it affects us. In reality, what we are
saying is that what they went through matters, and it
changes us, to be better friends, family, and neighbors.

A lot of people will say, "I'm here if you ever need me." A
better response is actually being with that person, giving
them time to feel safe with you, and inviting them to share
their story. If they refuse, let them know it's completely
okay, but reaffirm that what they experienced matters to
you, and that what you see them going through has affected
you. They don't have to share their story for you to help
them. Simply being there is often all they need.

Most people who say "I'm here if you ever need me" are
similar to the person who "liked" the Facebook status of
my friend who posted, "This is the worst day of my life."
My friend wrote back to the person who "liked" their post
and said, "Um, why did you like my post?" If you know of
someone going through loss, and if you really want to help,
be there---don't just say you'll be there. If you're waiting

for the loss survivor or victim to ask for help, you've likely already missed your opportunity.

Feeling Stuck

One of the greatest challenges with gaining influence is whether that influence should be used to stick up for yourself. On one shoulder, you have the "Stand up for yourself!" and on the other "Just let it go. Don't be a jerk." These internal interactions are quite common with individuals who have experienced loss, and especially for those who have been abused as children, because if they did speak up, they were silenced, ridiculed, punished, or feel guilty.

Take a moment and consider the last time you were driving and behind a line of cars at an intersection with a stop sign at each side of the intersection. After waiting for several cars to make their passage or turn in front of you, it now seems like it's your turn. But wait. You have to judge whether the cars to the left, right, and across from you reached their stop first. So you second guess yourself, and the other cars bullet by. Now, you reason, "it's my turn." By now, other drivers who reached the stop sign on the other side of the intersection see that you are unwilling or unable to go. They accelerate, causing you to step on the brakes again. It now feels like you are out of turn, and you're hesitant to drive forward because you're unsure what everyone else will do. To make matters worse, you have a driver behind you who is impatient and starts to honk their horn. "Go, already!" you hear someone shout. You've had it, pressing on the accelerator only to narrowly miss getting hit by another car. "I'm never going to do something that stupid again," you reason.

This is exactly what happens with those who struggle with meeting their Influence need, including everyone from bullied children to adults oppressed by their spouses. You wait to say something, hoping to be clear when it's your turn, only to have others' needs and voices zoom past yours. When it gets to be too much to bear, you finally share what's on your mind, but it feels like it's out of time, and the reaction of others (and perhaps yourself) is, "That was stupid." It only reinforces to you that your voice, and your influence, are not welcome.

One of my college students told me she had been the victim of constant bullying in her high school years. She felt that the comments directed to her were unwarranted and untrue, so initially she overlooked or ignored them. But the incessant bullying continued, and it started gnawing at her. At one point, she defended herself and yelled back at her accusers in the classroom. What was the result? The teachers started seeing *her* as a trouble-maker, someone who disrupted class and appeared easily agitated. She felt that "out-of-turn" sensation that accompanies so many people who struggle with sharing their influence.

As mentioned earlier, if you don't feel safe, you probably don't feel like you can talk about your needs. This is something loss victims and survivors know all too well. You don't feel comfortable sharing your fears, and so you live with them, often alone. Or perhaps there are those who *only* want to talk to you about your loss, and never seem interested in the "you" before or after your loss. To them, you no longer have hobbies, an identity, skills, anything—just loss. They always want to talk about your loss, but you don't want to because you don't feel safe with them or the topic. You need to know you are okay with or without the loss—and those who define you by the loss—although well-intentioned—keep saying to you, "You're not safe." We feel it more than hear it from those who either avoid talking with us or want to talk about our loss all the time.

Complaining

Whereas some people keep things bottled up, others are so focused on their loss that it's all they talk about. Some even go to great lengths to ensure that others will feel sorry for them because that means they were heard, and that they had influence on their listeners. Complaining brings with it a certain power, and even though it's negative, it's hard to not listen to it. If you have someone in your life who complains a lot, you have some options. The first is to turn them away or ignore them, but that usually leads to hurt feelings and lost friendships. The second is to say, "You know what, I really care about you, your life, and what you're going through. You have so much influence on me that I really need you to share more positive than negative things with me." Wow! Can you imagine? You just gave them the greatest gift in the world, and in the process, gave yourself one too. You helped them feel safe and now they know they have influence.

If you are the person frequently complaining, understand that how you communicate may not be interpreted the way you'd expect. One of the best practices for being more aware of how others view your comments is by developing a statement of "mindfulness." Linda Graham, author of *Bouncing back: Rewiring your brain for maximum resilience and well-being* defines mindfulness as "paying attention to the experience of the moment" (p. 52) while being nonjudgmental of that experience. For example, when you catch yourself complaining to another person, imagine yourself as an outside observer, perhaps someone you do not know, casually walking by, hearing your comments and watching the person who is listening to your complaints. You might think, "It looks like that one person has some anger issues," and again, "The other person listening to the complainer looks like s/he wants to get out of there."

Look into the mirror for a few moments, and then focus as much energy on the hurt you are experiencing. You will likely notice your facial muscles tightening, the mouth forming a frown, and the eyes filled with rage. That is the image others see; you may feel hurt by your experiences, but others may instead see an angry person and may prefer to avoid your company.

Comparably, when we complain about *ourselves*, it can be just as harmful as when others criticize us. Some of the vilest hate speech exists when we criticize ourselves. The source for this is often a built-in faux sense of morality that has developed from years of observing our parents, teachers, leaders, and with how we interpret those experiences. If these authority figures were often critical, we develop an inner voice, or thoughts, largely reflective of those memories. Those voices of shame or criticism are there because they influence us, and limit our own abilities to influence our world and others around us. This is why, at the moment when we feel the need for greater influence, we revert to the very voices that had such an influence on us. We see them as powerful, but in the process, they strip us of our energy and confidence.

Inner Critical Voices

Some popular trends fuel the belief that we bring upon us whatever we think, including poor health, accidents, and even death. While there is certainly truth that our thoughts often serve as precursors to our actions, assuming that everything that happens to us is what we attract, or deserve, is problematic. Many of us ask ourselves or a Higher Power, "What did I do to deserve this?" The answer to this question, in most tragedies, is absolutely nothing. It just happened, or in other cases, people made terrible choices that affected you or your family. Good parents of wayward children, having children or parents dying an early death, and being kidnapped or abused as a child should not be made to feel that they deserve their loss.

Yes, we are accountable for our thoughts and actions, but not everything in life is a direct result of our thoughts or actions. And while thinking positively or negatively will often lead us in a particular direction, life isn't always fair or perfect in what it gives or in its proportionality to what we think we deserve. This concept is important to understand if we are to have compassion for others and acceptance of ourselves irrespective of our circumstances.

Some people find that another option for dealing with negative thoughts is a simple but powerful redirecting technique comparable to the Emotional Freedom Technique

(EFT). One possibility is, when recognizing your inner thoughts being critical of yourself, say inwardly or out loud, "Even though I'm thinking critical thoughts of myself, I accept the positive qualities about myself." Another may be, "Even though I'm not feeling very good about myself right now, I choose to deeply love myself." Some individuals combine tapping, or using their fingers to tap on energy areas, while repeating the affirmations. When I am stressed, I sometimes tap each cheek as quickly (but not too forcefully) as I can until the tension leaves. It is a simple and silly exercise, but it does seem to work for me.

Andrea, a middle aged woman who experienced frequent sexual abuse as a young girl, was estranged from her parents early in adulthood. She recalled her first experience with "tapping."

> *In a midst of a class of peers (as a young adult), my body started shaking and going out of control. I had never experienced a panic attack before, but to the best of my knowledge that's what it was. A friend of mine asked me if I was okay, and I shook my head "no," and she helped me get outside. As soon as the door closed I started crying hysterically; I was in the bathroom (where I was abused) for all I knew at the time. My friend helped me with the tapping on areas and all I remember her saying was, "Even though" several times. It was the weirdest physical sensation I'd ever had. It felt like she was hitting me with a brick made of pillows; it was weird, but like a buffer of energy. It wasn't hurting me but rather relieving how I was feeling.*

Some individuals find relief from intense fear and stress by placing essential oils, such as peppermint, clove, and frankincense on their neck (over their thyroid) and on their back (over their adrenal glands). (Note: Be careful, as oils can sometimes irritate the skin; use a carrier oil and do not drink the oils unless you are absolutely certain it is safe to do so). Regardless of your technique, these re-directions of negative energy and thought will not likely be easy, especially early on, but over time, you will get better at it.

Humor

Some people look to meet their Influence needs by developing a sense of humor from the tragedies they went through. This sense of humor comes with a new perspective, sometimes a unique perspective, for looking at things and people's experiences. I have often heard that many of the famous comedians borrowed material from their own painful pasts to create humor. The challenge, of course, is ensuring that your sense of humor, or Influence, is not used in a way that puts other people down at the expense of a joke.

Years ago, when I was battling round after round of medical issues, I went to see a doctor for a follow-up appointment. The progress on my health was not as good as either of us hoped. After venting some frustration and acknowledging how much stress I had been under, including how I was unable to do all I should for my work and family, the doctor turned around and sat next to the table, writing a prescription. *Here we go again,* I thought, *more drugs that don't work.* When he handed me the prescription, it read: *Tropical Island Vacation. #7 days + 7 nights. Refill as needed.*

It's time to give yourself permission to be free of stress, even if temporarily. Give yourself a day, hour, or even 10 minutes as often as possible to just laugh and have fun.

It may not always seem easy to give yourself permission to have fun, but if Dortha Hise can do it, you can too. Dortha woke up one morning to realize she had permanently lost her voice from an auto-immune condition called abductor spasmodic dysphonia. Losing her voice meant she could no longer order at a drive through or over a counter, use the phone, or scream for help, and she now depends on her husband to introduce her in social situations. A sense of humor, "thick skin," and close family and friends have all been essential.

> *I have not let any of those things hold me back. While it has been about a year and a half, I have adapted everything in my life. I use Skype and Google Hangout to conduct my meetings, and I type while the other person talks. If I want to dine alone, I go prepared with thick skin that it's going to likely be challenging. I try to point and have all of my "sides" and "add ons" ready, but it's still a challenge.*
>
> *My sense of humor has really helped me through this. I'm able to laugh at so much more than I would have a year and a half ago when this was still fresh and extremely painful and sometimes even embarrassing. I went into Taco Bell for a friend and myself and I had decided to write down our entire order, because I thought it would be easier. As I*

handed the cashier the order, she looked absolutely
terrified - like I was robbing the place! Oh my gosh
- I started laughing and had to wait for her to make
eye contact to let her know I didn't have a voice. I
kind of pantomimed it out, but I didn't mean to
scare her. So now I'm more careful and start my
notes with, "I have a vocal disorder and..." and
always include a smiley face. I figure robbers don't
typically include smiley faces.

Talents

Another way to build our influence is through our talents.
Unfortunately, in our society we tend to place talents in a
box or with a particular label. *That person is an athlete,*
another is a musician, and another is a leader in the
community. If talents are, by definition, what we're good at,
then there is much more talent in our world, in others, and
in ourselves than what we typically consider.

Some have the gift of making others happy, others make
great listeners. Others have the gift of compassion. Often,
the very thing that we feel holds us back or down in life is
actually the source of our talent.

Shameeca Funderburk was six-years-old when she was
placed in the foster care system because of her mother's
challenges; her mother often left Shameeca and her two
little sisters for long periods of time. Early experiences
made Shameeca grow up fast, having to take care of her
younger sisters. When she was a young foster child, she
very much wanted to help her foster parents in their store.
When a customer was at the checkout area, and nobody
else was there to help the customer, Shameeca went behind

the counter. Shameeca recalled the following: "The customer couldn't see me behind the counter. I was young and too short. I didn't know my foster father was watching, but the customer gave me a $20 bill and I gave him the right change. After that my foster father gave me an hour every day behind the counter." Shameeca had developed a talent of taking care of people and being responsible, but it went from being a necessity for the safety of others in her earliest years to that of being something she wanted to excel in with the store.

Being Influential Doesn't Mean Influencing Everyone

Our Influence need or stage largely depends on whether the influence we have is valued by those we care most about. The number of persons we need to influence differs; for some, it may be hundreds of friends, and for another person, perhaps they only care what one close friend thinks of their influence.

Sometimes the best place to exert your influence is on yourself, and the most accessible method for doing this is through goal setting. Consider what is important to you and hold yourself accountable for taking every step possible to reach that goal. In reality, holding yourself accountable is a way of influencing yourself, or telling yourself to be or do a particular thing, and having your body and circumstances mold to that will.

Another creative outlet for sharing your influence with yourself is journaling. Many people use their journal for a sounding board, and very commonly, to complain or criticize others. I encourage you to use that time for deciding what kind of influence you want to have on yourself, and how you will accomplish those goals. At the same time, it is often better to direct your complaints at a journal than to lash out on others.

One of the dangers for desperately wanting to have influence is that sometimes those who feel they have too little control in their lives end up controlling others. If someone is seeking to control or manipulate you, you can always let them know that you welcome their influence, but not their control. Of course, if you are in a dangerous circumstance or relationship, you will likely need professional assistance and/or social support for making decisions that will best benefit you and your well-being.

NOTES

Graham, L. (2013). *Bouncing Back: Rewiring Your Brain for Maximum Resilience and Well-Being.* Novato, CA: New World Library.

Pelzer, D. (1995). *A Child Called It: One Child's Courage to Survive.* Deerfield Beach, FL: HCI.

Shakoor, S., Jaffee, S. R., Bowes, L., Ouellet-Morin, I., Andreou, P., Happe, F., Moffitt, T. E. & Arseneault, L. (2012). A prospective longitudinal study of children's theory of mind and adolescent involvement in bullying. *Journal of Child Psychology and Psychiatry. 53, 3,* 254-261.

Chapter 6: Value

Knowing we are important, loved, and belong are three components of a successfully resolved "Value" stage. While the Influence stage brings appreciation or respect for what you do, the Value stage brings appreciation or respect for who you are, your identity, core values, and roles.

Many times, the two stages are closely connected. Those with great influence, achievement, and contributions will tend to be valued by others. However, there are always exceptions to that rule. If you ask yourself why others don't value you when you have done a great deal for your family, employer, or community, then you may notice the disconnect that can occur between the two stages. Below are hypothetical examples to describe one who has successfully resolved the Influence stage but not the Value stage.

I feel comfortable talking about other people or things, yet I get nervous when others are focusing their attention on me.

I am confident completing tasks or assignments at work, but feel anxious when others ask me what I do for a living.

I enjoy talking to people I do not know, but then I tend to get nervous when they want to know a lot about me.

I feel fine when talking to others at my work about job-related functions, but then feel uncomfortable when giving a presentation because everyone seems to be staring at me.

We are literally programmed as humans to want to know that we are of value to others. Oxytocin, the hormone which has received a great deal of media attention, is a stress hormone that makes us feel good; as we feel positive approval and connection with others, our levels of Oxytocin increase, and our sense of happiness improves. It literally motivates us to connect with others to increase our sense of worth and value.

Those who have experienced loss and have felt rewarded for connecting with others after that loss tend to cope best. Unfortunately, many loss victims do not fare as well, at least initially. Many have said, "Now I know who my real friends are" because those with whom they felt closest to and valued by (before the loss) are no longer "there" for them (after the loss). The pain from those losses and sense of abandonment override their motivation for connecting with others, and in an effort to avoid future pain, isolate themselves even further. To them, the message is clear: They do not hold the Value they once had.

Self-Talking

Unfortunately, many times the inner voices of those experiencing loss are quite negative, and in my interviews with counselors and other professionals across several countries, I often hear about clients who wonder if they are "okay," if they are acceptable, and if they are enough. These pleas for validation are their last line of defense against their own inner thoughts telling them they are worthless. Dr. Samantha Madhosingh, psychologist and life coach, explains this challenge for clients:

There's a lack of faith in themselves. "I'm not worthy, I don't deserve it." It becomes so engrained in their psyche that they are undeserving. That is the biggest battle of all, that they can have faith in the idea that they deserve to have more than they have at this point.

Our Value doesn't need to be determined by everything that happens to or for us; it is much better and more stable when it is determined by our own perception of the talents we have, the skills we have developed, and the meaningful contributions we have provided to others. Let's take a moment for an activity. Take two minutes and list all of your skills, talents, and awards you have ever had. Set the timer. Ready? Go!

---------	---------	---------	---------
---------	---------	---------	---------
---------	---------	---------	---------
---------	---------	---------	---------
---------	---------	---------	---------

Did you complete the list? Was it easy or difficult? We should often think of the positive traits we have, and why we value them. The more you value what you have (or can do) rather than what you don't have, the more you will value yourself.

Consider a shy woman who has a difficult time connecting with others. If she focuses on that limitation in her life, she will feel of limited value. If, however, she is able to notice other things she is good at, then her value will not be as impacted when she is in situations that tax her shyness. At the end of the day, she can say, "Well, perhaps I wasn't very good at talking in public, but I am good at all these other things."

Robert Brooks and Sam Goldstein, in their book, *Raising Resilient Children*, refer to these characteristics as the "island of resilience," where individuals have at least one thing they're really good at to buffer them from those moments or things they are not so good at. Many people focus on their own limitations, and try to hide them or focus a great deal of energy on improving them. While improving on limitations is a good thing, a more effective strategy (especially after loss) is to build upon our strengths.

When you went in for a job interview, did they ask to see your resume of weaknesses? When you really wanted that job, did you tell them, "Well, sometimes I have poor handwriting and I can get easily discouraged"? Similarly, our lives and successes are better predicted by our strengths than by our weaknesses. Chances are there are strengths already in your life that could bring a great deal of happiness if you give them a chance.

Valuing Your Loss

In addition to determining what you are and do are of value to you and others, an important step in building your sense of value is by recognizing the good that has stemmed from your loss. Your loss is an important part of who you really are, and trying to hide or deny its impact is essentially minimizing your value.

Earlier in this book, you were provided with an activity (i.e. Language of Loss) to help you see how your loss has negatively affected you. And for many, our loss is what we focus on. But loss is a learning experience, a growing experience, and one that forces the recipient to change.

Of course, this doesn't mean that you have to like that your loss occurred, but it does mean there is a need to embrace what it has taught you. It is a part of you, and when you value how it has or can change your life, then you will learn to value yourself even more.

Seeds of Change

Have you ever heard someone say they "feel like a million bucks"? As mentioned earlier, feelings determine where our needs are. When you wake up in the morning, do you ask yourself what you're worth? Many people do ask that question, and the outcome of that answer leads too often to depression, anxiousness, and doubt. They doubt life will ever give them anything better than they already have. They don't feel of worth, and they don't feel worthy of receiving anything better.

In a previous chapter, I shared a little about Liana Luna who felt abandoned by her parents, and how that lack of safety affected her. One of the turning points in her life happened when she made the decision to stop using drugs.

> *We went in and met with the director of a program and shelter, and the director asked me questions. One of the rules is that you are six months clean and sober (before being accepted in this program). I literally had two weeks clean and sober. I was asked, "If you only had two weeks sober, what's going to make me take this chance on you?" I said, "I've never tried to stop, and this is my chance." He replied, "I'm going to take a chance on you."*

> *What I remember about the people there is that they're not there to preach to you, or convert you. They are there to feed you, talk with you, and not judge you. That's one of the biggest things I remembered about the program…that selflessness. I renewed my faith in humanity. Living in the drug world for so long, I believed everyone does something for something. It was so refreshing. I renewed my faith in the goodness of people and the world.*

Liana now works for a school helping homeless children and their families, and has been clean and sober for many years. She has also been able to reconnect with her children after she had been homeless and in jail earlier in her life.

Liana's experiences demonstrate how important other people can be when someone is trying to develop their sense of value. While I believe her support group literally served as a miracle for her, I can also see that it was her commitment or decision to change that served as a catalyst for that miracle; if she had not committed to change, the miracle would not have materialized. Not only did others take a chance on her, she took a chance on herself.

This sense or willingness to take steps or make changes, even when you are uncomfortable, is often the result of having a clear vision for you are and who you can become because of that loss. Dr. Tony Paulson, a therapist and colleague of mine, describes it this way:

> *Those who stick it out have a clearer focus for what they want their life to be....the story in their mind of what they want their life to be. Those who can engage in treatment recognize their life was meant for more, and they have that internal drive to realize that potential.*

Karen R. Koenig, LCSW, M.Ed., who, like Tony Paulson, helps individuals with eating disorders, finds that the vision or value of oneself often serves as a filter for all their other experiences. When they say, "I'm so overwhelmed" or, "I can stand it," it's essentially telling the brain that they are of no value or worth. According to Karen, the way to resolve this lack of worth is by changing the meaning of one's experiences, similar to an earlier chapter's discussion on reframing. Karen works with individuals who have internalized a lack of worth based on how their parents treated them, and Karen often helps her clients understand that it was a lack of parenting skills, and not a lack of love, that many of these parents had for their children. Their loss becomes less personal, and becomes more of a learning or growing experience.

The Self-Esteem Myth

Our culture is saturated with books, motivational products, and drugs (legal and illegal) to help individuals feel better about themselves, even if temporarily. Although feeling good about ourselves is a positive thing, the methods have been temporary, distorted, and lacking. The media, politicians, and academics have perpetuated the myth that if a person just feels better about themselves, then the right kind of behavior will follow. In reality, it is far from a predictable connection.

The self-esteem hype was at a climax in the 1960s, a time of heightened drug use among teens and young adults. It was also a time of increased distrust (i.e. consider the first stage of the Potential Framework) of the government and other authorities, including parents. In response, millions of dollars went to programs designed to improve self-esteem among youth, with the expectation that increasing self-esteem would lead to decreased drug use. What was the actual result? The interventions and programs increased the self-esteem of youth and drug users, but they did not change teen or young adult drug usage. Drug users with low self-esteem became drug users with high self-esteem.

Despite these and other contradictory results on changing a person's self-esteem, we believed what we wanted to in society. What had once been seen as a means to an end became the end-goal as our society wondered what we could do to improve a person's self-esteem, and we continually assumed that if high self-esteem was reached everything else that was good would follow. Not only have professionals bought into this myth; advertising and our very way of life seem to perpetually recycle the belief that the ultimate goal is to feel good about ourselves. We buy the newest and the best because it makes us feel important, at least until something newer comes out.

Another reason our culture and science have focused on self-esteem is that it's easier than many other personality or psychological traits to improve upon. Obtaining or experiencing anything important or positive will likely improve a person's self-esteem. Self-esteem can also dip suddenly because of the loss of those very things.

Tying Your Value to Things That Last

Rather than obsessing about whether the girl or guy you have a crush on smiled or frowned at you, or if someone you admire gave you a compliment or was critical of you, it's more important to tie your emotions to symbols that last. This point was driven home for me in my early years in academia, as I was involved in collaborative work on a study about body image. What we found was that female teens and young adult females who tried to emulate a role model's talent or intelligence had better perceptions of their own body image than those who most wanted to be like the women who are most known for their looks and body figure. This study also reminded me of the importance with tying who we are and what we want to be to things that really matter.

Children's TV Programming

Do you remember your favorite TV program as a young child? Nearly every parent can recall at least part of the theme songs from these children's shows. What made these shows so popular had little to do with the special effects or believability of these programs, but rather their ability to make children feel wanted and needed. They feel loved, they feel safe, and the characters even invite the viewers to talk to them (e.g. "What's your name?") and make decisions (e.g. "Where do you want to go today?").

There is a great deal of good in meeting these needs for young children, but I think there is also a great deal of danger in having these needs met primarily through technology. Do we wonder why children, when they grow up to be teens, close their doors and engage in nonstop texting and social networking? Or when they seek to imitate sexual violence found in the media? Technology is a great forum for communicating, but I think there is an epidemic of our children being raised by computers and the Internet.

Your Value, Alone

We often measure our Value by our money, assets, opportunities, and relationships. Each of those things (and especially people) are important, but if you feel you have lost everything or everyone of value in your life, now is the time to believe in your value independent of everything and everyone. That value often arrives when we learn from our loss. Whether you have a great or failed marriage, the respect or disdain from others, or money (or lack thereof) in the bank, there comes a time when you are forced to face the real you. For Georgiana, her test occurred following a third divorce. Afterward, she came to a stark conclusion.

> *The divorce made me take a long look at myself. I*
> *had to do some self-examination because this was*

*my third marriage. I realized my mistakes. I needed
someone to complete me and when he did not
measure up to what I needed I lost interest. Now the
divorce has been final for eight months. What I
learned is that when you are broken you will attract
broken people, so before you get married make sure
you are a whole person; it will save you years of
heartache and suffering. Life is too short to not be
happy.*

Loss always comes with a price tag, and it will always
exact its cost, but growth occurs after we choose what we
will do or be because of that loss. Loss can make us feel
value-less, but it can also force us to consider ways for
improving ourselves. Much like Georgiana and her divorce,
Chris also experienced a divorce and it forced him to
improve his life and who he was.

*My divorce was filed five years ago, and I was
forced to represent myself. I took the stand planning
to tell the truth and allow the court of law to work
its magic. That was a mistake as my words were
twisted around to make me appear abusive.
Immediately following my ex-wife filing the divorce,
my life was in pieces. One night I looked up at the
stars to realize how many there are. If there are this
many stars, think of the planets that orbit the many
stars and of the life that inhabits this expansive
number. How much do my problems really matter in
the grand scheme of it all? Ever since, I have done
much self-discovery, I have done much in the way of
personal development through a devoted meditation*

practice, and began the first university recognized chapter of the National Coalition For Men to address Men's Issues.

Notes

Brooks, R., & Goldstein, S. (2004). *The Power of Resilience: Achieving Balance, Confidence, and Personal Strength in Your Life.* New York: McGraw-Hill.

Chapter 7: Investment

There is a tendency to stop and consider what is most important in our lives when we are experiencing loss. Cemeteries are instant reminders of what is really important; it's not just living, but how a life is lived. Gravestones are all about how we have invested in others, and not the other way around. Have you ever seen "Here lies the guy who was treated well by others" on a tombstone? How people view our lives is ultimately determined by how we treat others, and less by how others treat us. While death may remind us of that, the lesson is for the living.

Once we find a sense of Value, or have our basic needs met, the greatest source of our happiness comes by what we do for others. Indeed, research has found that, after having enough money to pay for food, clothes, and housing, having more money bears no correlation with being happier. Of course, this doesn't mean money isn't important, but once we are secure in our own needs, if we are going to continue to grow in our potential, our focus needs to be on helping others.

This lesson was reaffirmed for me when my Uncle Don died. It was a time of reflection. I realized that the memories of Uncle Don I held dearest after his death were the same ones while he was living. There was no need to idealize when he was already consistently a certain way. Uncle Don was consistently kind. I'm not referring to spoiling or buying attention or love, but he had a knack for being interested in the details of people. It left a huge impression on me, and made me wonder about the influence I'm leaving with those I care about most.

Recalling the Potential Framework

The difference between the earlier needs (i.e. Safety, Influence, and Value) and that of Investment is a major shift in focus from the "me" to helping others. It is going from "I want you to keep me safe, and help me know I'm here and important," to "I am here to help you change your life for the better."

As we progress through the Potential stages, we become less egocentric (focusing on ourselves) and more altruistic (focused on helping others). We can help others begin their healing and progress toward their potential. We can be the kind of person *we* needed when we were going through our loss. We can give them a better chance for a brighter future. Gregory Gass, who works with adults and teens experiencing trauma and pain, explains it this way:

> *Almost always the person who was traumatized, but thrives, had someone or something to cling to that gave them hope. They can look back and there was some adult in their life that stood out as a consistent figure of unconditional love for them in the face of their plight. It might have been a grandparent, aunt, uncle, teacher or coach, but they will describe someone who was always there for them.*

The Danger of Not Investing

Investing in the lives of others helps them move through the stages of Safety, Influence, and Value, whereas a lack of Investing in others can have devastating consequences.

Not getting involved in others' lives may just be the difference between life and death. How many times have we heard of people not getting involved when someone really needed help?

Fortunately, there are also those who are willing to help, as I witnessed when one of my neighbor's children went missing. My neighbor's autistic child, who was 8 years old, had run away from home. Our neighborhood quickly became involved and invested long hours in the search efforts. News crews filled our street, and an Amber Alert sounded throughout the community, petitioning anyone who may have seen the boy. The questions started to surface: *What was he wearing? What does he look like? Do you have a picture of him?* One of the key pieces of information was that he was riding on his scooter. Actually, all of the information was vital. A little over seven hours after the boy's disappearance, he was found miles from his home, hiding in a construction area under a conveyer belt. Fortunately, he was unhurt and returned home to his parents.

I also often think of the bravery of so many people during what has most commonly been referred to as "9-11," when a string of terrorist acts rocked the United States. There are countless stories of heroes from the fire and police departments, and also from common or ordinary people, who chose to make extraordinary decisions to help others despite the risk to their own lives.

The consequences of not getting involved, or investing in the lives and welfare of others, usually do not lead to life-or-death circumstances, but it still feels that way to those who need your investment and do not get it. For them, the details matter. Being interested in their lives, their hopes, ambitions, and struggles shows them they are safe and have influence and value. Not being involved in the lives of those whom you might influence may have serious mental, emotional, and relational consequences for those who need your care right now.

Investing as Parents

Which parent would you rather have, one focused on meeting their Influence/Value needs or one who is looking to fulfill their need for Investment? The one who is frequently looking to meet your needs or one who is chronically absorbed in their own "selfie" moments? What kind of teacher, employer, supervisor, coach, or clergy would you prefer to have? Which would *you* prefer to be? Growing up, we may have idolized those who put all their time into themselves, but those who really made a positive difference for us were those who were willing to give of, and sometimes give up, their resources for our own well-being.

A good example of this was illustrated in May 2014, when Kevin Durant received the Most Valuable Player (MVP) award. Rather than brag about himself, his wavering voice was used to thank his family for their investment in him. Just days before Mother's Day, he gave a special tribute to his mom.

> *Everybody told us we weren't supposed to be here. You woke me up in the middle of the night in the summer time. Making me run up a hill. Making me do push-ups. We weren't supposed to be here. You*

made us believe. You kept us off the street, put
clothes on our backs, food on the table. When you
didn't eat, you made sure we ate. You went to sleep
hungry. You sacrificed for us. You're the real MVP.

Parents are often known for their sacrifice and investment they make for their children. Time, money, energy, and other resources all go into wanting to see their children safe and happy. A pregnant mother may change her eating habits, take vitamins, and eliminate alcohol and smoking just so her newborn baby may have an increased chance at better health.

Whether we are parents or not, we are all lifelines for which others depend upon. The choices or decisions we make to improve the lives of others are examples of our Investment in their well-being.

Investing in Others

Lisa Ford-Berry, whose son was bullied and committed suicide, told me of her need to invest in the lives of others, even if she could "help just one person to not go through what I did. I understand their fear, and they need an advocate." That hope and sense of purpose of helping others provides energy and confidence in life.

For Karen Krolak, who experienced the loss of three family members in a car accident, her act of investing consisted of sharing the seeds from the tomato plants her brother had grown.

> *The (plants') vibrant hues and odd shapes made me*
> *smile and reminded me of how my brother could*

sneak levity into the most solemn or saddest events.
I packed up several different varieties in a plastic
container and clung to the idea that we would plant
them once we were able to move in to our new
home.

Simple Acts of Investing

Sometimes investing or advocating for others is a relatively
simple task. In a *New York Times* column, Bruce Feiler
summarized research that had one question: "What is the
biggest predictor for the stability and happiness of your
family?" The answer, according to Feiler, is to build a
strong family narrative, or "words that bind." Telling
stories about their birth, your life, and the lives of those
family members who had lived before is an important start,
but the emphasis was on the moral or lessons learned.
We're a family, and we'll always stick together. You matter
to me. You're part of something big. We've gone through
tough times before, but we'll make it through; we always
do. These stories, narratives, and morals teach others they
are safe, had influence or meaning, and that they are a
valuable contributor to that story.

Of course, not all stories are complimentary. Sometimes
they tell the recipient they are different, unwanted, or the
butt of other's jokes. If the investment is going to be a
positive one, it must have a positive message, and we are
urged to consider how we tell these stories. Whether you
are a parent, a spouse, a sibling, or friend, look at the
stories you tell (or don't tell) as a sign for how you invest
in that relationship.

Another simple act of investing in others is simply caring, which can be both an emotional and more importantly, a behavioral, response. In their work on resiliency, Robert Brooks and Sam Goldstein found that the strongest predictor of whether a child would become resilient is if they had at least one caring adult in their lives. The semantics of the word are important, in that the child must *know* that the adult cares for them, and not just that the adult feels that they care for the child. Many times these caring adults are known as mentors; not ironically, mentoring often creates stronger resilience in the mentor as well. In the words of Dr. Samantha Madhosingh, "Giving back is healing on so many levels for those who have experienced loss."

If you want to know how much you really care, count the number of compliments you gave yesterday. Can you remember each compliment? Only count each as a compliment if you are confident the recipient *knew* it was a compliment, and if you didn't expect *anything* in return for that compliment. Write each of those compliments below.

--------------- --------------- --------------- ---------------

--------------- --------------- --------------- ---------------

--------------- --------------- --------------- ---------------

Now, divide the total by the number of friends, family members, neighbors, and associates (combined) you interacted with (via phone, social networking, texting, talking in person, etc.) yesterday. That number or result is the average number of compliments you gave to each person you interacted with yesterday. If your average is less than one, say .4, that means you gave, on average, four-tenths of a compliment to each person. I'm not sure what four-tenths of a compliment even looks like. (Can you imagine living off four-tenths of a compliment each day?)

Again, compliments are only compliments if they are genuine. Giving compliments because it's on a checklist or because you want to ensure your own morality is comparable to giving a pretty gift box with nothing inside. In contrast, a genuine gift inspires hope, no matter how it looks on the outside, and requires nothing in return. A genuine gift is a transfusion of courage. It is also a strong method for building trust and helping others feel safe.

Other simple acts of investment deal with taking a chance. Over the years, as my children have grown up, neighbors have taken chances by hiring them for various types of work. My children have worked in a variety of settings, including yard care, taking care of quail and dogs, babysitting, and helping neighbors move. It not only reinforces the life lessons of hard work and responsibility that we (my wife and I) teach them, it also tells them "I notice you. I value you. I trust you." These experiences have also taught my children to trust themselves, that what they do matters, and more importantly, who they are matters. Of course, children don't need to receive payment to help them move through the Potential stages, and neither do adults. Sometimes all that is needed for individuals is a listening ear.

A simple act of investment may include preparing a video or letter with you telling them why you are grateful for them. Many times, especially if we are an authority figure, such as a parent or community leader, we assume we need to use the video or letter to tell them what they need to do. Telling them how much you appreciate and love them will have more of an impact, and if you do offer advice at the end of the video or letter, it'll make your recommendations even more important to them.

Altruism

Investment is often purposeful, and the general idea is that you hope others will benefit from your investment. But sometimes we can get so tied up in looking for the result or outcome of our emotional investment that we can lose sight of the value of those we are investing in. If we are seeking to affirm our Value through our Investment, then we have it all backwards.

Altruistic behaviors are those for which we give, and give of ourselves, with no thought of reward. No strings attached. When was the last time you visited a nursing home on Mother's Day and helped strangers feel better? When was the last time you gave money to a family anonymously during the holidays? When was the last time you called up a company just to tell them that the employee helping you that day was efficient and kind? Our personal potential hinges more on what we do to show we care than simply caring.

In reality, there is nearly always a reward or string attached to being kind, and it is the warm feelings we receive when being kind to others. But when you say, "I'm going to do this regardless of the outcome, whether it's appreciated, and whether others know it was me," then you are investing for altruistic reasons.

This is a powerful tool for those who have experienced loss because it helps us get outside ourselves, outside the pain of our own experiences, and focus on the strengths we have that can be used to help others. It is truly about increasing and reaching our potential as we help others.

Investment Priorities and Balancing

One of the hidden dangers for the Investment stage, especially for those who have experienced loss, is overcompensating in a particular area in their life. They can invest so heavily in their work, service, advocacy, religion, or other parts of their life that they lose track of other things and people that were important before the loss occurred.

I had a student who was passionate about learning about anxiety, as well as how it affects academic performance. Most students exhibit some level of anxiety toward tests, papers, and big projects, but on the day her assignment was due, I could tell she was really struggling. I was very worried about her and tried to calm her down. "I can't do it," she replied over and over. Her passion (and self-selected assignment) was to learn everything she could about anxiety, and focusing so heavily on her challenge likely made her life even more challenging.

Like this student, many times we assume the things we are passionate about overcoming will be the same things we are passionate about pursuing, investing time in, and helping others with. There is no doubt that many of whom I interviewed did exactly that, but a successful Investment in those things usually requires us to feel safe, have influence, and to know we are of value *first*. When individuals invest their time into their fears without first meeting those earlier needs, they often feel more fear.

I've also known of parents who were not as involved in their children's lives as much as they would like to be due to investments in their employment, military service, mental health, or other reasons. These parents often experience regret, guilt, and even shame, which sometimes motivates them to invest in others rather than in those they're closest to.

These alternative parental investments feel good because they are providing the feelings you wish you had with your own child, creating a sensation that all is not lost. But these kinds of investments can also be a form of denial if they are done for the purpose of making up for lost time, relationships, or identity. They may also create an additional rift with those who are seeking your attention, affection, and approval.

Here are three questions you can ask yourself if you are struggling with the Investment level:

1. Have I met my earlier needs or levels?

2. Is the issue or problem that I am investing in the wrong thing/person, or is it that the way I'm investing needs revision?

3. Are my Investment expectations realistic?

Investment Careers

Many of the social work, family services, and other compassionate care careers are filled with those who have experienced some kind of loss. Although this has been the trend for some time, I believe it has gotten even stronger, and compared to the "Be Objective!" mandate of professionals in the past, more professionals are recognizing that their own experience makes them empathetic to the needs of those they serve. Vironika Tugaleva, author of *The Love Mindset*, also noted this in her email to me:

> *I think this is the emerging trend with people-helpers in our generation. People want someone who's been there and back, someone who knows more than theory.*

Consider Tom Gagliano, keynote speaker, and author of *The Problem Was Me*, who experienced a transition from dealing with loss to that of helping others because of that loss.

> *I became a bully as a kid, and later as a recovery addict. But I sabotaged all the relationships in my life. You saw me as a successful person on the outside, but inside I was experiencing a slow death. My wife and children left me, and I had a decision to make. Either I was going to fix what was broken inside of me, or I was going to subjugate myself to a very lonely life. I knew I didn't come from a good childhood, and went in for therapy, and had two goals: (1) To give my children what my father couldn't give to me, a safe place to share their*

feelings, and (2) to help others who, like myself,
who suffered from destructive childhood messages.

Advancing technology has allowed for a variety of fields, professions, and methods for helping others. Keep in mind the importance for resolving your own loss before entering these careers so that you do not re-traumatize yourself. Additionally, whether you are entering or maintaining a career that centers on loss, you should be able to affirmatively answer the following question: Are you going to allow anything good to come from your loss?

NOTES

Feiler, B. (March 15, 2013). The stories that bind us. New York Times. http://www.nytimes.com/2013/03/17/fashion/the-family-stories-that-bind-us-this-life.html?pagewanted=all Link accessed July 17, 2014.

Gagliano, T. (2011). *The Problem Was Me: How to End Negative Self-Talk and Take Your Life to a New Level.* Carefree, AZ: Gentle Path Press.

Karen Krolak. http://bootstrapcompost.wordpress.com/2013/08/30/delicacies-from-the-dregs-the-spirit-of-life-compost-and-rebirth/

Kevin Durant's MVP Speech (2014). *https://www.youtube.com/watch?v=mqEL51Cfad0 . Link accessed July 17, 2014.*

Tugaleva, V. (2013). *The Love Mindset: An Unconventional Guide to Healing and Happiness.* Canada: Soulex Press.

Chapter 8: Acceptance and the Power of Letting Go

Not accepting the past is the emotional equivalent of holding onto a big rock with both hands while trying to swim in deep waters. The rock may be "solid," but that doesn't mean you can depend on it to get you through. We too often hold onto things that are hard, instead of letting go. We tell ourselves we can't get by or get on top of our problems, and so we hold onto the thing that is always there—our pain.

At some point, we need to convince ourselves, emotionally and mentally, that all we can do is indeed all we can do. We can't go back to the past or forward into the future; now is the time to do the best with what we have. Give your own inner child the words of wisdom you wish you had received. "It's okay if you weren't perfect. You tried hard. You worked hard. I am so proud of you. Your failures, hurts, and frustrations are only a piece of you, and you can let them go. I accept and love you for who you are right now."

Let's accept who we are, even when we are looking to improve, or as one person told me, "This whole time, I was searching everywhere in an attempt to find who I wanted to become, forgetting that the most important place to look is already inside of me." Developing a sense of meaning, or more specifically, a positive meaning and purpose are essential if we are to accept and let go of the past. According to Patrick Wanis, human behavior expert and life coach, learning to turn our loss into an asset is "about giving meaning to the loss and what that meaning is. It is about what we are going to learn from it so that we become a different person, because we can never be the same. That leads to asking what I can do differently to lead a happy, successful life."

Earlier I wrote about the need to focus more on our positives than on our negatives, but once we feel safe, have influence, and feel of value, we can also feel secure with reaching into our faults and limitations and are ready to tackle them head-on. Acceptance and "letting go" doesn't mean being neutral or passive, but it does mean we recognize what is real and decide where to go from there. Acceptance and letting go are powerful tools for succeeding the *next* time. If you miss reaching a goal, or are stopped short of a dream, acceptance helps you let go and try again or to try something else that may be even more rewarding.

As a father of three children, including one preparing to "leave the nest," my wife and I recently looked at each other and asked, "What happened to the parents we wanted to be?" In the earliest years of our children's lives, we were determined to be a *particular kind* of parents. But things changed. We did have moments that fit our expectations, but there were many times when we have not been that way. Finances, chronic health problems, setting up needful boundaries, and adjustments to just "keep us going" have made us the parents we needed to be, but not necessarily always the parents we initially wanted to be. Having that discussion with my wife was hard; that dream meant a great deal to each of us, and not fulfilling it felt like we weren't good parents. It was personal. But we look at it, and see what we have learned, who we have become, and more importantly, what our children can learn and how they can grow from it, and it helps us accept the past but still live in the present.

You could also consider the resilient first grader who studied hard only to have his exam returned to him with marks indicating he got 51% of his answers right. When the teacher looked at him sternly and asked, "Do you understand what this means?" the student replied, "That I got most of them right?" Chances are high that you and I have done some really dumb things, but we got some of it right too, and that simply has to be enough.

Why Acceptance Fuels Future Perceptions

Not accepting the pain from your loss is the surest recipe for remaking or recycling that pain for you and for others. Without that acceptance, you are driven and blinded by your desire to recreate circumstances to fix that pain. You'll seek out situations and people that give you another chance, another opportunity to repair the damage that may have happened long ago. That teen girl who hadn't fully accepted the pain of her distanced father is now a wife or girlfriend driven toward interactions and affections with those who remind her of her dad, or the pain of that loss, desperately seeking their approval.

The boy who grew up without his mother's approval is now a husband who looks for his wife to make up for the loss of a mother's love. When his wife is unhappy, it must be because of him, because he needs to be the center of her world; when he is unhappy, it must be because of her failures. Or the boy who grows up feeling unsafe with his father later becomes a father himself, and has anger issues with his children that have more to do with his own childhood relationship with his father.

Incredible conflict ensues in these kinds of interactions because each person interprets the same experience through different perspectives, and these perspectives are largely formed by their own most pressing need. *Why am I the bad guy when I am working so hard? Why do you think I'm cheating on you if I'm friendly to the opposite sex?* Our sense of what is right or okay, for our own actions as well as for others, is largely influenced by the need or level of the Potential Framework we are trying to meet.

This is particularly true for those who are parents and have experienced loss of their child. A parent who has experienced her child's death, who craved to have more of an influence on that child in life, may seek out relationships and experiences that provide an outlet for the guilt she feels. Every chance she gets, she talks to parents about how they can be a better parent, while she has another child at home who desperately needs her attention. The thing to recognize is that, regardless of the type or time of loss, wanting to meet those needs is not a bad thing, but that we are all prone to focus exclusively on meeting our own needs resulting from our loss to the detriment of other needs, people, and relationships.

Accepting that loss, or accepting the pain from that loss, is telling ourselves, "I accept that pain. That pain is there because it tells me it's okay to want to feel safe, to influence, or to feel of value. I accept how it has affected me. I accept it may be with me for a very long time. I'm not

116

in charge of what others have done to me in the past, but I am in charge of how I deal with these emotions from now on."

Lisa Ford-Berry is one of those people whose stories initially motivated me to write this book. Lisa is a good example for accepting loss and pain, as she realized how it molded her into someone who could help others. Despite the traumatic bullying and suicide of her son, and the silence of those who stood by while her son was bullied, she recognized her loss and pain as core parts of her identity, and she was able to find acceptance through her faith.

> *"It took me two, maybe three years, to get anything out of my faith. But I will say, five years later, it is much richer, deeper and different. I believe to the depths of my being, it is the reason why I am able to forgive, truly forgive. I know at the end of my life, I will see Michael again. It took a long time to work to that. When you talk about compassion, I think those of us who have suffered are able to understand in a way others who have not suffered cannot."*

The last sentence shows that loss or the pain from that loss can become a strength. Of course, this doesn't mean we go around wishing for trauma, but once it happens, it will change us forever. Acceptance puts that change into perspective, and it allows closure on our pains and loss.

Bryn Barton, also one of my first interviewees, shared with me how her journey toward acceptance and forgiveness was forged as she learned more about other people's trials. After some time in complex trauma therapy, and hearing the accounts of others who had also experienced trauma, Bryn began to realize how powerful the forces were that ignited people to do bad things. She cited how some troubled individuals have generations of role models who show or tell them what to do, and now it's their turn to provide for their family, and violence is all they know.

Again, accepting the pain is not the same thing as saying that what others did to you or what happened was ever okay or ideal. Rather, it is exchanging the *focus* on that pain for the *willingness* to grow. Accepting that pain, that hole in your heart, is the first step to gaining the emotional reserve for forgiving others.

Although acceptance is easier and more complete when you successfully resolve the previous needs, the Acceptance stage or level also threads and intertwines with all the other levels. How do I fully meet my safety needs when I cannot be completely safe? How do I meet my needs of Influence when I am an introvert? How do I Value myself when others do not seem to value me? How do I meet the Investment need if others do not use or appreciate what I have given them?

The answer is that we learn to accept where and who we are. No strings attached. Or more precisely, to accept ourselves because we *do* have strings (our faults and weaknesses) attached. Acceptance puts things in perspective, and it will tend to make loss, regardless of the stage or level it impacts, a piece of you and not the whole you.

Perfectionists have incredible talents. They have dedicated their lives, and each day, to the pursuit of perfection. But the one thing perfectionists have difficulty with is acceptance. Ironically, it is the inability for perfectionists to accept others' imperfections that limits their own potential.

Recall that the primary process for increasing and reaching one's greatest potential is by transitioning through the stages in the order provided in this book. Perfectionists seek to maintain trust and safety through order and by minimizing mistakes, but when that sense of order is disrupted, the only person they may trust is themselves. Perfectionists' investments in others may be made to reinforce their own value (or how others view them) and less on increasing the value of others. In this sense, perfectionists may be attempting to reach or increase their potential by going through the Potential Framework in reverse order.

Many perfectionists also struggle with telling others "no." They take on added responsibilities and tasks for helping others (i.e. "investing") because they feel that telling others they can't or won't do something will ruin what others think of them (i.e. value). As I'm writing this, I'm reminded of my very first car purchase for $300. It was a 20-year-old coupe, and it was a horrible tint of yellow. The floor mats could not cover the holes on the floor of the car, and as I drove I watched the road pass underneath me. When I went shopping, sometimes shopping carts would hit my car, and others would apologize for "dinging" my car. I simply let them know I couldn't tell a difference, and as a

119

matter of fact, it may have even improved things. Of course, there is nothing wrong with wanting to look good and to have nice things, but it is equally (and sometimes more) important to "let go."

The key for perfectionists is to understand that trust will need to be strongly developed, not only for themselves, but for others, before they are able to develop their greatest influence and true value. It is that sequence that will help them better learn to "let go" of the things that are not inherently essential to their happiness.

I do not have a vendetta against perfectionists. The reality is our world would have not gotten as far as it has without their help, and there is no doubt we will continue to rely on their services. If I need a job done at my work, on my car, or on my home, I would probably want a perfectionist to be in charge. And I admire the fact that a large percentage of perfectionists are not hypocrites; they apply the same standard to themselves as they do for others. My point is that perfectionism is a "loss," one that the holder of its characteristic misses out on being able to develop meaningful connections with others and within themselves. Consider the following excerpt from Stephani, who struggled with perfectionism for two decades:

> *I define perfectionism as the inability to be vulnerable and letting the mental construct of how I should be vs. who I really am get in the way of participating in life and having fun regardless of what's supposedly expected of you. Perfectionism is a trap and it totally sucks.*

It started when I was 15 and a freshmen in high school. I put on 20-30 pounds in less than a year and felt the sting of comments from upperclassmen boys. I decided I could buckle down, exercise, eat less, and lose weight. Within a year I had transformed myself into a "hot sophomore."

However, I was stuck in my own perfectionist prison and unable to connect with people and make friends. I felt awkward in my new body and the attention I received and experienced the "imposter syndrome" at its worst. [People] thought I was a snob rather than someone gripped by fear and self-imposed isolation. I wanted to break out of it but I didn't know how.

By age 35 I was stuck in a bad marriage to a man who ignored me, belittled me, and isolated me from friends and family. He pushed me to live within the constraints of his perfectionist and strict religious doctrine. I quickly saw how wrong it was and that I was living a double life, literally, between work (which was fun) and home (which was stifling). After two years and a lot of mental pep talks and prayer, I found a way to start running and taking care of myself. Through this time away from him, defiantly taking care of my unworthy self, I found strength, confidence, and clarity to leave the relationship. To this day, I believe that my perfectionist isolating mindset attracted more of the same and led to meeting and marrying this man.

I now allow myself to fail, I go out with unwashed hair, no makeup, etc. and let my home have comfortable clutter, and even more than that if I am stressed and overwhelmed by life. I feel much freer now and look back on the time between age 15 and 35 as the lost years.

Aicacia, who had also struggled with perfectionism, explained her perception of perfectionism this way:

Perfectionism, to me, is the fear of mistakes and flaws mixed with an obsession of appearing flawless all the time. I also feel that it's a mild form of pessimism that teaches you to focus on the negative aspects of life instead of the positives.

Gratitude

Many of us have heard the expression of having an attitude of gratitude. Our level of gratitude determines our altitude in life. Research has shown that those who are grateful tend to live longer, healthier, and happier lives. But is this a chicken and egg argument? Do we need to live a long time, be healthy, or more successful in order to be grateful? Or can we be grateful despite our circumstances?

My grandmother lived her childhood through the Depression, and had just about every known catastrophe piled on her. One of her daughters experienced debilitating conditions as a child, and all four of her children died before their 55th birthdays. Her husband developed symptoms of Parkinson's, and then cancer, before he lost his life. She also had severe anxiety when speaking in public. But when you talk with her, you'd think she had just won the Lottery. She was grateful, not only for everything, but in every condition. "I'm so grateful for my blessings," she often said. I believe this sense of gratitude buffered her from many of the hardships that she went through, and she was a source of comfort and confidence for others, including me.

As a struggling father and husband, I had little direction in my life. One of my greatest fears at that point of my life was that I would not be accepted into a PhD program. I was a country bumpkin who often felt intimated in an academic setting. And I had to score high on a GRE test before starting the program. The night before taking the GRE I visited my grandmother and told her how nervous I was. "Oh," she replied, sounding matter-of-fact-like, "you'll do just fine." She then got out a deck of Pinochle cards, a game she had played for over 50 years, and for whom everyone in the area knew of her skill. We played several hands until I earned enough points to win the game, and she went out of her way to tell me that the cards "were just there" for me. I knew better, but it was her way of saying the best cards would be dealt to me when I took my test the following morning. She was right, and I scored in the 93rd percentile on the exam, earning a $12,000 fellowship along with free tuition. I often smiled when I told her that card game was a $12,000 card game. "The cards were there for you," she always replied with a smile.

Gratitude comes easier for some than others, but it is something we can all cultivate. If you struggle with being grateful, the best place to start is a gratitude journal. Wake up in the morning and write down five things you're grateful for, and before you go to bed, write five more things you're grateful for, avoiding repeating or copying early comments. Finding new things to be grateful for is the key to rewiring your brain into seeing the best in you and others.

Gratitude is not only a mindset for what you have, it is also a bridge for getting where you want to be. Have you ever been jealous of a family member, friend, or colleague who seems to have the best looks, the greatest fortune, or the best of luck in their lives? It is almost as if our emotions convince our minds that others are stealing our chances for being happy. We start to see those as excuses for our own failings. But what if we could cultivate an attitude of gratitude for their success? Doing so would free up all that negative energy and time invested in feeling sorry for ourselves, and use them for moving forward in our lives. When we are grateful, others want to be around us more, and we begin to get more done. Others will start to appreciate us more, leading to the same kinds of breaks we initially wanted but couldn't get because we were going about it the wrong way.

Adapting

When many of us think about "acceptance," we assume we are accepting what is, and sometimes it seems like a passive word. But true acceptance is more about adapting than it is about neutrality. For Shelley Rafilson, adapting wasn't easy, but it was necessary. Like many people in this economy, Shelley lost her job, and that loss was compounded by other losses. Here is her story of tragedy and triumph.

I was seriously hurt at work a few years ago. I was a legal secretary for over 25 years and fell down as a co-worker had asked me to help her find something on her computer and did not let me know that her desk area had files to watch out for on the floor that were hidden but that one could easily slip over. I tripped and fell down and developed severe Neuropathy from the fall. I was later laid off, supposedly due to the economy when layoffs were occurring because of that. When I called the EEOC in Washington, I was told that was happening a lot, that elderly or injured employees who companies did not want as staff anymore, as they were considered liabilities due to ill health or injury, were being let go with the excuse of economic layoffs. So unfortunately for me, after seven years at a firm to which I was dedicated and a hard worker, I was shown the door under the excuse of economic layoffs.

It was a very difficult time for me. I now had severe Neuropathy and was living in constant pain. I also had Fibromyalgia. It never affected my work status but was worsened by this new condition. My beloved father, who was also my best friend, was partially paralyzed on one side due to a stroke and he lived in assisted living. I helped take care of all of his needs making sure he got out and enjoyed life as much as he could, and I handled taking care of all of his personal needs, while now not well myself, on my own, and struggling to get by.

I ended up gaining over 100 pounds and was using NSAIDS for severe Neuropathy pain. My father, through his positive spirit, inspired me and I was able to lose over 100 pounds and stop using NSAIDS for pain. I now use more natural means for pain. With everything going against me, in my 50's, in menopause, on medications that can cause weight gain, taking care of my father on my own, and seeing how he had to live with partial paralysis, besides just struggling to survive, I changed my mind set, was positive, and turned my life around.

I wrote and published an eBook and book entitled "100 Pounds to Happiness!" about my journey, helping to inspire people through my story. My father passed away in March 2014, and is the book is dedicated to him, as is my CD. Now that my health has improved I am also working on pursuing my singing career again.

Besides the financial devastation it caused, I was physically hurt and personally hurt. I learned that life goes on and we have to adapt no matter what. I am hoping to help many others through my book about my experiences to remain hopeful and positive. I am also working to find success in my music career again. I am in my 50's but I have a positive mindset and believe we should never give up on our dreams. Sometimes things happen in life and we have to find a new direction but keep on going.

Forgiveness

Can you reach the Acceptance stage without forgiving others or yourself? This is a sincere question with a very complex answer. The reason for its complexity has to do with how we define "forgive." If you're like me, you typically see forgiveness as an act of finality, or being able to let go and never return. While there are certainly some people in my research who have experienced this, it's more common for individuals to revisit how and why they can or should forgive. It is more of a process than a destination.

Tiffany Mason, relationship and life coach, and author of *The Power of Adversity- A Guide To Finding Your Greatest Gift In Life*, was sexually abused as a young adult, and found the power of forgiveness as a relief from the burden of hanging on to those memories.

> *It has taken me a lot of time to really think about this [forgiving]. I would not be where I am today if I did not forgive this man. I know it seems kind of strange because he did this horrible thing, but you can't move past a traumatic situation if you can't forgive. If you don't forgive, you'll always have that in the back of your mind. It's that burden you carry on a daily basis. I do forgive him, and I'm able to really live my life the way I deserve, and away from that burden.*

Another interviewee told me about her process, and the challenges that came from it, for forgiving. She compared it to getting "pop-ups," memories and emotions triggered throughout her life to remind her that those issues still needed to be resolved.

When I first started teaching on a university level, a female student came into my office for some advice on an assignment. It was near the end of the semester, and I noticed that she had worn sweat pants and a sweatshirt every day to class. She looked like an athlete, or at least I assumed she was an athlete. After giving advice on the assignment, I asked what sport she played. She answered that she didn't play any sport. Without me asking about her attire, she quickly shared the reason she always wore sweatpants and sweatshirts. When she was in high school, and getting ready for the prom, her mom advised her to not wear a particular dress. When the teen daughter asked her mother why, her mom said she thought her date would think she looked fat in that particular dress. This student had reportedly been wearing sweatpants and sweatshirts ever since to hide who she was.

This student's experience broke my heart, not only because of the damage that can be done with just a few words, but because focusing on that memory gave her little room and energy to focus on other things. She was afraid of who she was, and she was afraid of how others would perceive her.

For years, I have taught Parenting classes to college students, many of whom are passionate about *not* becoming the kind of parent their parents were for them. It often took an entire semester before they realized that their negative emotions concerning their parents were essentially throwing the baby out with the bathwater, as they focused on one of their parents' negative traits, characteristics, or events and overlooked the examples of good from their parents.

Similarly, one of my friends in graduate school was abandoned by his dad when he was a young boy, and once my friend became a dad, he committed to being the best dad ever. The challenge for him was that he had focused so long and passionately on what he didn't want to become (i.e. like his dad) that he had little direction or specifics of being a good dad. His incessant requests to his wife about, "What should I do? Am I doing this right?" became so problematic that his wife asked him to work even more hours rather than spending that time at home. If we are focused on the negative, we become at greater risk for repeating it. If we focus on what we could improve upon, or how (specifically) to strengthen ourselves or others, then we are likely to do just that.

And who can forget the story of forgiveness with a class of Amish girls in Lancaster, Pennsylvania, being gunned down by a neighbor in 2006? Although the media tends to focus on the negatives or trauma of a story, this had a much different and deeper meaning, as the Amish community reached out to the shooter's family to offer their forgiveness the day after the shooting, and even attended the funeral of the shooter who committed suicide.

Also consider Chris Williams, author of the book, *Let it Go*, who publically forgave the teenage drunk driver just weeks after he crashed into Chris's car, killing Chris's wife, his son and daughter, and his unborn baby. One of the news stories described how Chris was able to forgive.

> *Williams had essentially trained — in the way a marathon runner might start with leg exercises and shorter runs — so that when the time came to forgive the nearly unforgivable, he was ready. ---*
> *(Deseret News)*

At the age of 6, Shameeca Funderburk's mother left Shameeca in charge of her two younger siblings. The police eventually got involved, and Shameeca and her sisters were taken from their mother and placed into the foster care system, where she lived with foster care parents who helped push her in the direction she wanted to go. I asked Shameeca about forgiveness and acceptance, and here are her comments:

> *That took place when I was about 33. It was more of a spiritual thing that helped me do that. It was through praying, and for the first time, I was able to start thinking about myself. I also started thinking about my mother [and the life and sickness she had to deal with]. I was able to call and forgive her, or at least I left a message because she didn't answer and if I didn't do it I knew I wouldn't do it later. It's not that I'm angry or frustrated, but I'm not used to having a mother. We talk more now but it's still awkward, and it may take time, or it may never happen. I've accepted that.*

Forgiving Yourself

Sometimes the person to forgive is yourself. I had the fortunate experience of interviewing Jeff Olsen, author of *I Knew Their Hearts*, who, while driving, lost his wife and youngest child to death, as well as a leg from the accident. He grieved for years while trying to understand, "How do I turn back time? How do I get it all back?" For Jeff, what helped him forgive was a series of spiritual near-death experiences over several years to convince him that "everything was in divine order," and that what had happened to him was for his ultimate good and growth.

Each story of loss illustrates how letting go of the past is important to our emotional health. For most of the individuals I interviewed, many of them talked about how forgiveness was a process, something they chose to do but that it usually took a lot of time and required them to do it many times, largely due to the "triggers" discussed in earlier chapters.

A Whole New Level

A person who successfully resolves their needs for Acceptance will then revisit their needs of Safety, Influence, and Value, but this time with a different purpose and greater resolve. Each new time after successfully transitioning through the Potential Framework, we gain the skills and confidence to succeed where we are. If you learn to meet your Acceptance needs, you may revisit the Safety level, but with the express purpose of strengthening your sense of trust even more.

Many times, acceptance and the process of letting go lead to the realization that loss is not what life is all about. This is often a long process because our loss can appear to take up every minute of our lives.

For Jane Robinson, who experienced complete hair loss, including body hair and eye lashes, in her middle-aged years due to Alopecia (an auto-immune condition), the realization of what life was really about was a process, and one that became incredibly rewarding. After multiple doctor visits, various treatments, hiding her head with a wig, feeling unattractive, and experiencing discouragement and stress, Jane decided there was more to life than the difficult emotions she was feeling.

> *Early in the morning, I wrapped a scarf around my head, and took a walk on the beach. It was one of those mornings when I was watching dolphins jump, children running out to catch the waves, and older couples holding hands. And then I realized, it hit me, this is life. It's not about your hair, how you look, or even how people see you. I decided I was going to live a life that was more authentically me. It was going to be lived, and lived with my soul. Over time, my hair grew back. It wasn't my original hair color. It was white. And I loved it.*

Learning to accept herself and realizing her loss wasn't what defined her was something Julie Smith, a single mother who counsels teens and parents, could relate to as well. Julie experienced her parents' divorce when she was 13, and she experienced a series of loss events, including her own divorce, a miscarriage, and the death of her mother-in-law whom she felt a strong emotional connection with. For years, she tried to suppress the feelings that came from her early loss, but after the death of her step-mother, it forced her to deal with all the loss she experienced. When she learned to accept the loss, both the loss of people and relationships from her loss, as well as the grief of what those people and events meant to her, her life became much richer.

> *I had this shadow of loss that kept following me. I just ignored that loss but then I lost my step-mother, whom I had a strong emotional connection with. Losing her led to questions. That loss shook me. She truly believed in me. It felt like a 2X4. I could no longer ignore how these loss experiences affected me. It affected everything – my work, parenting, and how I saw myself. It hurt my health, because I had a heart condition, and it made it worse. I was sobbing and thought, I can't do this. I can't go around it, under it, or over it. I've got to go through it. I have to grieve all loss in my life. It was incredibly hard. I had to change and embrace that change. I had to feel I had to have a reason to be here, a purpose. I realized whatever I had been doing earlier wasn't working. I hadn't previously felt good about myself. I looked successful on the outside, and yet inside I felt like I was falling apart. I realized I was creating the tension in my life when trying to deny the loss. How I was dealing with all the losses in my life just*

wasn't working anymore. I was angry with God, myself, everybody. I had to allow myself to be angry.

I had to let myself go through it, and it helped me teach my kids that it's okay to feel and to share what they feel. The more transparent I became, the more I started to know myself. The more I knew myself, the more transparent I wanted to be. And then I realized I've gotten to this place where I know me and others connect with my story, but I wanted others to connect with me. I didn't want to be my story. I know I'm not always status quo, and I'm okay with that. I couldn't say that before because I thought I'd be judged. It's just been in the last year that it's okay with me.

There is this childhood picture of me. I look at it and I look at her eyes and there is sheer bliss. I feel like I am that person again. I have confidence.

Did you notice the process involved in Julie's transition? It entailed learning to trust her own feelings of grief (Safety), to be able to share her feelings with others (Influence), and eventually to a point where she valued who she was in a more complete way (Value). She accepted how loss changed her, and it brought her to a much richer sense of possibilities and confidence than had she not worked through the steps we now know as the Potential Framework.

NOTES

Quote taken from
http://www.deseretnews.com/article/695239655/A-year-of-forgiveness.html?pg=all . (Let it go). Link accessed July 17, 2014.

Mason, T. (2015). *The Power of Adversity: The Guide to Finding Your Greatest Gift in Life. CreateSpace, South Carolina.*

Olsen, J. (2012). *I Knew Their Hearts: The Amazing True Story of a Journey Beyond the Veil to Learn the Silent Language of the Heart.* UT: Cedar Fort.

Section 3

Chapter 9: Potential Revisited

As a child, one of the things I wanted most was to live up to my potential. I knew my parents were watching and wondering if I would do all I was capable of. Now, as a parent, I want my children to live up to their potential, but I realize it's okay if there are stumbles along the way. I just want them to be happy, and I believe finding and living up to their potential is how to find that happiness.

Having Your Best Day Ever

Almost every day when I drop my children at school, I leave them with the words, "Have your best day ever." I'm not exactly sure when or why I started saying that, but it's become a habit. It tells them I want them to look for the best in their day, and I want them to leave the day better for them and for those around them. Even if they are experiencing difficult circumstances, I want them to make that day all that they can. To me, that is happiness. I have often found myself saying it to others as well, wanting to pass on a sense of optimism.

Years ago, my wife and I wrote a book about hundreds of youth entrepreneurs (and their parents), many who started their businesses following a tragedy. In their teen years or even earlier, several youth were inspired to do something great, and for many of them, that is encapsulated into their business endeavors. The fact that a teen could build and run a business is incredible enough, but when it is done after experiencing trauma it is truly remarkable.

Their sense of resiliency, or making something good happen from something traumatic, isn't only possible, it's absolutely necessary.

If your inner thoughts keep telling you that you'll never amount to anything, decide it's time for a change. You will still likely have those thoughts, at least initially, but the more positive thoughts you create, the less negative thoughts will be able to influence you. This process will take time, patience, and (hear the piano teacher say) practice, but it's worth it. When you develop mostly positive thoughts you will say to yourself, "It's not the size of the obstacle, but the strength of my thoughts." If you focus on negative thoughts, you're going to think "It's not the size of the problem, but how little I really am." Decide which approach is more likely to help you grow and commit to it.

Stop thinking, "If I could only survive this" because it's not enough, and start thinking, "What greatness can come from this?" You are on the trampoline of life, and whatever has gotten you down can eventually bring you much higher.

Your emotions are signals letting you know if you are on track, whereas the way to change your life is by changing your thoughts. This is also why emotions determine which need you have, but changing your thoughts will determine whether you increase your potential or not. The key is to learn to change your thoughts, and your emotions and potential will follow.

Many times we assume we have to develop complex strategies, elaborate mantras, or take expensive medications

138

to change our thoughts and improve our circumstances. Sometimes what we need is much more simple and accessible. Sometimes we just need to remember.

In a series of experiments conducted with German college students, the authors of the study were interested in "self-generated emotions," or emotions individuals recalled from past experience. In the study, they asked students to recall a memory filled with happiness; and at different points in time, they were asked to think of a memory filled with anger, then another memory that made them anxious, and yet another that made them sad. They also asked students to remember how they usually felt when brushing their teeth to serve as a baseline. After each memory recall episode, the students were then given various tasks, such as pulling an object, throwing a ball, and jumping. Once the experiments were complete, the researchers found that recalling happy and anger-filled memories led to the students' best scores in each of the experiments, and recalling anxiety and sadness-invoking experiences led to their lowest scores.

You may be reading the previous paragraph and thinking, "I understand the link between happy thoughts and potential, but what about angry thoughts or memories? Are you suggesting I get angry each time I want to reach my potential?" To answer that question, we should further ask ourselves why people get mad. We may respond with "they're frustrated, tired, hurt, or stressed." These answers represent the effects and not the real cause. Not everyone who is frustrated, tired, hurt, or stressed shows their anger toward others. But those who get angry at others, including yelling, belittling, or even physical responses, such as hitting or shoving, do so because it's effective at getting what they want. More simply, it works, at least temporarily. This is why those who manipulate, yell, criticize, or hit others keep going back to being angry after promising to change.

In a sick and sometimes hurtful way, those who frequently get angry are actually reaching what they perceive to be their potential, but their potential is always measured by what they can make other people do. In the long-run, this will lead to a loss of real friends, loss of trust, and greater isolation, fear, and loneliness. That is their true potential until they change their ways, starting with changing their thoughts.

Coming back full circle, the study about athletic or physical performance relates to much more than our physical ability. It relates to everything we want to do in life. It also provides us with a simple technique for strengthening our potential, especially for those who have experienced great loss, by intentionally anchoring our thoughts to memories that bring that greatest happiness. It will not only increase our present potential, it will also protect our emotional and social well-being while helping others improve theirs. Focusing on the memories eliciting angry emotions can never offer all those benefits. The study also emphasizes that how we feel is a choice. Having your best day ever is most likely when you anchor your thoughts to the experiences and emotions that lift you, and let go of those emotions and experiences that bring you down.

Increasing Our Potential Never Means Pushing Others Down

I believe in the ability and accountability of each person to make their lives better than they received it, and by focusing on the Potential Framework, they make their lives most rewarding by helping others. Conversely, we can never increase or reach our full potential by making it harder for others to reach theirs. Pushing others down will never help us find our true potential.

Pushing others down is not the same thing as standing up for yourself. If there are people who limit your ability to feel safe, have influence, or feel valued, there may be times when you need to tell them that what they are doing or saying has an impact on you. Presentation and tone are just as, if not more important than, the message you want to send. Remember, when standing up for yourself, explain how fulfilling your needs will improve your relationship with that person, group, or organization. (Please note: If you are currently being abused, please seek professional assistance as soon as possible. Many who are abused feel it is their fault, and there is nothing further from the truth).

The idea of "potential," truly understood, is indeed one of the most compassionate things we can give to those who have been hurt. If we learn to recognize what needs we have by our emotions, we also learn to climb through the sequence of needs by developing the right thoughts.

To be safe, have influence, to know our value, to invest in others, and learn acceptance are principles any person and society need to have if we are going to develop, expand, and attain our potential. If parents, teachers, clergy, and other professionals are looking to help those who have dealt with loss, I believe it is by helping victims and survivors better understand who they are and what they are capable of. Victims and survivors also need to recognize that the cycle of hurt and pain can stop with them. They can teach the next generation how to better cope with loss, as well as to "have their best day ever."

Do I Take Care of Me First or is That Selfish?

Nearly everyone has been confronted with the question of whether they should focus more of their time, energy, and emotions on personal healing or "lose themselves" in helping others. It is a difficult question to answer. We have two polar opposites, whether coming from our own mind or the rest of society, with one telling us to take care of ourselves first, and the other telling us we need to take care of others first.

Even though it may not feel like it, this tug-of-war between these two forces is quite good for your sense of humanity. It means that you care about others and you care about you. It also means you believe your contribution to others is important. The challenge, of course, is making decisions that prioritize one person or group of people over another. It is also difficult because you know someone may be disappointed.

A useful method is to consider the Potential Framework in the context of the initial question. If you don't feel safe, in any way or with any one, then I submit that is the most basic need and being able to help others will be incredibly difficult until you meet that need. The more your basic needs are met, the more likely you should choose to invest your time and energies in helping others meet their needs. (Of course, this doesn't mean we have to have all our needs met before we should help others). Avoid the interpretation of you being "evil" or "bad" or "selfish" or "I deserve it," and focus more on the following: "How can I increase my potential?"

Pet Loss

In the preface of this book, I wrote about the power that stems from hearing from ordinary people who do incredible things, and why those stories are inspirational for each of us. But I think pets can often be seen as ordinary or usual, probably because they are largely dependent on people. When I asked individuals to share their experience with "pet loss," the response was really quite incredible.

Many people have developed strong emotional connections to their pets. I think the closeness many people feel with their pets is a reflection for how those pets meet the potential needs (i.e. safety, influence, value, investment, and acceptance) of the people who care for them. This is because many pets, especially dogs, are very protective of their owners, so that makes the owners feel safe. Many pets understand verbal cues and emotional changes of their owners, giving us an opportunity to share our voices, to be heard rather than judged, and have a sense of influence on those pets. Pets can also increase our sense of personal value, because even when we make mistakes, our pets still want to be with us and still like us. We invest in their well-being, and learn to accept them despite their idiosyncrasies, and they despite ours.

Tobi Kosanke's story of pet loss was heart-warming to me.

We found Bear on the side of a street in 2003. His pads had been burned from the hot pavement and he was unable to walk. He was at least 8-years-old, had parasites indicating that he had been surviving on rotten garbage and dead animals for an extended time, and cracks on his teeth suggestive of having chewed on a metal chain. With his intense gratefulness at having been given a loving home and his gentle demeanor with all of the people and animals he came in contact with, Bear quickly stole our hearts and changed our lives. While we could literally write volumes about this very special little Chow, one story in particular illustrates just how amazing he was. Although he did not have an aggressive bone in his body, in December of 2007 he successfully defended the farm from coyotes. He never turned his back to escape and he fought off the coyotes, alone, until he could no longer stand. Bear recovered remarkably quickly and when he was able to walk again, the first thing he did was revisit the sight of his fight and do a little "dance" on the spot as if to celebrate his success.

The following February, Bear had his senior exam and was declared "older than dirt" but in excellent general health. Our veterinarian warned us that, at his age - estimated to be at least 14-years-old - every day that Bear was still with us was a small miracle. Although we cherished every single day with him, we were ill prepared for the terrible void

144

*that was left in our lives when Bear passed away six
months later, on 8/20/2008, less than 48 hours after
showing the first symptoms of advanced lymphoma.
We are heart-broken at losing Bear and our lives
are greatly diminished without him. In Bear's
memory, we have had a sign made to hang on the
gate that Bear selected as his own for going into
and out of our pastures, declaring it "Bear's Gate."
Bear, thank you for the love you gave us and the joy
you brought us. We love and miss you more than
words can express.*

Experiencing pet loss inspired several of those who shared
their story with me to engage, or invest, in a cause that
helped them honor the memory of their pet. One person
created an organization devoted to "pet therapy," a practice
that helps comfort, guide, and befriend those in need
through pet ownership and training.

Parents aren't always clear whether a child is prepared to
take on the responsibility of caring for a pet, and these
concerns are valid and important to consider. The ultimate
goal, in my opinion, is whether pet ownership will help a
child reach their potential.

Metamorphosis

Loss changes us. We will never be the same. Whether we
change for the better depends on how well we develop our
potential. Whether our needs center on Safety, Influence,
Value, Investment, or Acceptance, we can always increase
our potential.

Potential takes you from a distrustful, "What can't I do because of my loss?" to a more hopeful, "What can I be because of my loss?" It changes the tide of energy from fear to trust, from being silent to being heard, and from feeling worthless to worthy. Potential helps you go from doubting your abilities to expanding them.

Some of the more analytical readers may wonder, "But who, exactly, in this book, reached their full potential, and how would you know that?" As mentioned earlier in the book, we all have the capability of continually increasing our potential, and "potential" is not a static thing. Each and every person I interviewed, in their own way and time, showcased a great deal of potential. I never, ever interviewed a person thinking, "Well, this would be a great example of how *not* to reach one's potential." They all experienced life, and were thrown some serious curveballs. But each showed incredible courage, resilience, and found a way to improve their life and the lives around them. They worked on their emotions and made their emotions work for them, motivating them to do and be ever better.

Run the Race

Sometimes the change that takes place from loss isn't what we anticipate. This is a lesson Jordan Hadley learned early in life. He grew up on his family's ranch in Ogden, Utah, and one day his dad was crushed by three 850 pound bales of hay, likely being the cause of a stroke that left his dad speechless and largely motionless. Two years later, after personally training a horse named Dreaming of Kisses, Jordan entered a race at 35:1 odds to win. Despite the odds,

Jordan and Dreaming of Kisses won Idaho's large horse race with a $100,000 purse.[2]

Like Jordan, we are all running the race of life, and it's difficult to know exactly where we will find our greatest potential. Loss may seem like an event that keeps us from our dreams, but it can also help us create new dreams.

Mental Illness

An unspoken assumption (and myth) for many is that living up to our potential equates to being free from distractions or limitations. Nothing could be further from the truth. Living our potential means accepting challenges and finding a way for them to make us stronger.

Unfortunately, those with mental illness are often perceived to have limited potential, even though, in many cases, having a mental illness actually requires more energy, more effort, and more courage than not having a mental illness. Those with a mental illness are not fated to fail.

In one study, 125 patients were seen for anxiety and depressive mood disorders over a one year period. The study's results suggest that having a mental illness does make the pathway toward resiliency and potential more difficult because there are more obstacles, but it also shows that there are certain factors to help buffer the challenges of having a mental illness. The first was a sense of spirituality, which generally refers to a way of looking at the purpose of their life in connection with others, and the second

---

[2] This story came from multiple sources, including People.com, KSL.com, and the Idaho Statesman.

recommendation was physical exercise. In the Potential Framework, and particularly among those with mood disorders, this fits well with the Safety stage or need, because spirituality (or a sense of finding purpose or meaning in experience) and exercise (to relieve stress) will help meet the safety needs.

In another study with depressed mothers, the intervention began with two separate groups: one for the parents and one for the youth of those families. Each of the groups fostered an atmosphere that helped make them feel safe (a process called "normalizing" of their stress) and were encouraged to share their experience and insights (i.e. Influence). Program facilitators were trained to validate emotions (i.e. Value), and participants were invited to take an active role in the direction of the group to determine what issues should be resolved (i.e. Investment). Preliminary results showed that the youth group's likelihood of developing "at risk" behaviors was cut in half, and mothers reported significant improvements in family togetherness, as well as substantial reductions in stress, anxiety, depression, and somatic distress.

Several studies have also shown that adolescent females are at greater risk for developing an eating disorder if their parents are harsh or unsupportive and provide little affection. Of course, some individuals develop eating disorders even with supportive parents, but the main idea is how important it is to provide a positive atmosphere, especially for children, to help them feel safe, be able to share their voice, and to feel of value.

These are just a few studies of many that would support the Potential Framework and they give hope to those who struggle with mental illnesses, eating disorders, or at risk behaviors. Given the individual, family, and societal effects of mental illness and other at risk behaviors, it is imperative and compassionate to help them with their Potential Framework needs.

Love

The Potential Framework may also be helpful when considering what "love" is. To those who are looking to have their Safety needs met, they will love those who keep them safe. For those who are seeking Influence, they will love those who encourage them to share their voice. And those do not feel of Value will love those who help increase their self-worth.

Our experiences with loss sensitize us to what love is or should be, and it frequently creates misconceptions and unrealistic expectations for marriage, dating, parenting, and other relationships. Your spouse or partner may be saying, "I listen to you, I value you, I buy things for you and give you my time, and I accept you for who you are," and yet you may still feel it isn't enough because you need to feel safe. Being able to articulate your need, and how to meet that need, is imperative for that relationship.

However, sometimes you may have to meet your own needs. Indeed, expecting a spouse, parent, or child to meet every need you feel at every moment of every day is nothing less than throwing darts at a moving dart board. For that relationship to grow, it must go through the various levels or stages; it's difficult to Invest your love in someone else if you do not Value yourself.

The Potential Framework not only helps us communicate our own needs with those we love, it also helps us better understand the needs of others. For this reason, you should be able to more fully appreciate your spouse, partner, or child for how far they've been able to grow. Are you able to look at those you care about through the lens of the Potential Framework? Can you identify their need to feel safe, have more influence, or to be valued more?

Morality

Comparable to love, morality also follows the stages of the Potential Framework. Someone who does not feel safe is going to have a different perspective of what is right and wrong than a person who feels of value. In an NBC News interview, Elizabeth Smart, who was abducted from her bedroom as a teen, said, "Things that I'd always told myself I'd never do, I would do them if it meant I would survive. If it meant that one day I would be able to go back home and be with my family again, I would do it."

If the goal is to help strengthen a person's sense of morality, we shouldn't judge them, because they cannot change where they cannot yet be. Helping that person feel safe, knowing their words have power, and knowing they are valued for who they are (and not be judged based on what happened to them) are three keys for helping others.

Although the Potential Framework may be helpful in understanding the choices people make, it is no guarantee.

Just because a person's Safety, Influence, and Value needs are met, they still have a choice for how they will act.

A "Potential" Table and Summary

Below is a table summarizing the Potential Framework. Following is a list of affirmations.

The Potential Framework

Need	Triggering Emotion	Those struggling with this need often
Safety	Fear/Distrust	Seek people and moments hoping to find a sense of security, but are often cynical of other people's motives.
Influence	Helpless/Hopeless	Feel their voice is minimized or oppressed. It may "build up," leading to out-of-time or awkward moments.
Value	Worthless	Wonder if they are important to others or feel a sense of belonging. In some cases, they may know they are needed, but they may not know they are wanted, liked, or loved.
Investment	A desire to protect, guide, or improve the lives of others	Overcompensate in one area they are passionate about and overlook how it may affect other aspects and relationships.

Acceptance	A desire for closure or ultimate growth, purpose, or meaning.	Do not want to let go of the hurt because they are uncertain of what letting go means to them.

Affirmations

Below is a script you can use to help guide your journey toward your own potential. Feel free to revise for your own personal use and needs.

I have great potential. I am not defined by my mistakes, but by my life's resume, filled with strengths, talents, and what I can contribute.

I am safe. Past experience, loss, abandonment, and pain. All of these things, and how I feel about them, make me human. But they are not there to make me lose trust. Now I will trust. I will trust myself that I will know whom to trust. I trust that my experiences, both wonderful and hard, make me more compassionate and knowledgeable for how to help others.

My influence is positive and welcomed. My voice is getting even stronger. I have permission to share my thoughts and beliefs, and I have a positive influence on my family, friends, and employment. I own my thoughts, but they do not own me. It's okay if others do not fully accept or like my influence; I am at peace with that. My influence is exactly where it needs to be, but as I progress, my influence will continue to increase.

My value is great. It is not diminished by pain or loss. Others may try to assess or diminish my value, but only I can determine what that value is. I commit to being of worth to myself and others on this day, and I open my heart to opportunities for healing and growth.

I am investing who I am and what I have to help others; helping others increases my own potential, as well as those around me. I will invest wisely, and understand the risks of that investment.

I forgive those who have wronged me. I forgive myself. I give myself permission to forgive and to let go. Forgiveness isn't saying it was okay or acceptable that someone got hurt. It is accepting myself and who I have become, and letting myself become even more.

NOTES

Rathschlag, M. & Memmert, D. (2013). The Influence of Self-Generated Emotions on Physical Performance: An Investigation of Happiness, Anger, Anxiety, and Sadness. *Journal of Sport & Exercise Psychology. 35 (2)*, 197-210.

Jordan Hadley's story.
http://www.people.com/people/archive/article/0,,204491 15,00.html http://www.ksl.com/?sid=12224864 http://www.idahostatesman.com/2013/08/03/2687124/the yre-the-kind-of-people-you.html

Min, J., Jung, Y, Kim, D., Yim, H., Kim, J., Kim, T., Lee, C., Lee, C., & Chae, J. (2013). Characteristics associated with low resilience in patients with depression and/or anxiety disorders. *Qual Life Res. ,22(2),* 231-41.

Riley, A., Valdez, C., Barrueco, S., Mills, C., Beardslee, W., Sandler, I., Rawal, P., (2008). Development of a Family-based Program to Reduce Risk and Promote Resilience Among Families Affected by Maternal Depression: Theoretical Basis and Program Description. *Clinical Child & Family Psychology Review. 11*, 12-29.

NBC News interview with Elizabeth Smart, who was abducted from her bedroom as a teen.
http://www.nbcnews.com/news/other/i-was-broken-beyond-repair-elizabeth-smart-recalls-kidnapping-ordeal-f8C11336267 . Linked accessed August 14, 2014.

Chapter 10: Limitations and Exceptions

Similar to any framework or theory, there are exceptions and limitations with the Potential Framework. When using the framework, be cautious about overanalyzing yourself and where you are at, or what level you need to work on.

Consider someone who is motivated to work on both Influence and Safety needs. It is possible a person may need to start with the lowest level to ensure it is met, but it is also possible that meeting the Influence needs may help meet the needs of Safety. The clearest example of this is an infant who is crying; is she trying to influence her surroundings or is she trying to meet her safety needs? It does seem that both needs are being met. As adults, we Invest in an occupation to ensure Safety needs are met. For this reason, the levels are not completely independent of one another, but I recommend giving the most basic need the greatest priority.

Between 1933 and 1945, Jews, who were held in concentration camps, were torn from their families, livelihoods, and communities. Despite threats and realities of harm and death, Jews used their voices to lift their spirits, to protest how they were treated, and to defy those who would dare try to break their spirits. They used what Influence they had even when their Safety needs were not met. They used their influence to state that no one, nothing, not even death, will control their thoughts. One song, Die Gedanken sind frei, translated to "My thoughts are free," was reportedly sung as they marched toward their deaths.

Some of the song's lyrics are:

Thoughts are free, who can guess them?
They fly by like nocturnal shadows.
No man can know them, no hunter can shoot them
with powder and lead: Thoughts are free!

And if I am thrown into the darkest dungeon,
all these are futile works,
because my thoughts tear all gates
and walls apart: Thoughts are free!

This song, as well as those who sung it in concentration camps, provide evidence of the resilience of the human mind, and the potential for each of us to be great despite the loss we encounter. But it also shows that the framework is not without exceptions. In general, the framework should be viewed as a map, and not the only road, for getting to where you want to be.

Our potential will vary across situations, relationships, and events. It is not a "got it" and "get done" kind of deal, but rather something we all can work on. Focus on one loss, event, relationship, situation, talent, or characteristic, and then consider how to increase or reach your potential for that one thing. Once you feel you have reached it, that would be a good time to start working on another goal.

Semantics

One thing that is less clear in this book, as well as in various fields of study, is what the difference is between a victim and survivor. Many use the terms synonymously, for example, to describe a young child whose parent dies; that child is technically a victim and survivor of that loss. In this book, I typically consider a survivor as someone who not only goes through the loss, but who went through something awful and they're still standing; survivors are resilient and who molded their tragedy into something that will help them and others.

It is also important to recognize that having some of the emotions and behavioral responses as another person does not make us an expert on another person's loss. Some loss victims and survivors may be especially offended if you claim you understand what they are going through. You may not completely understand the event or specific emotions, but you can understand some of the possible needs after loss. Our goal is to be involved and help others. In the words of Lisa-Ford Berry, founder of B.R.A.V.E, "Say something. Do something." Our acts of compassion help us reach our potential by helping others reach theirs.

For the Academic and Practitioner

There are many questions an academic or practitioner may ask of this new framework, and even of the research involved in writing this book. Two of the challenges of the Potential Framework, much like any framework or theory, are the semantics and symbols. For example, should the "needs" be referred to as levels, layers, steps, stages, or paths? While I tend to see them as stages, a strict theoretical definition of the word "stages" implies that individuals must go through one before going through the next, and as already indicated, there are exceptions.

Other issues deal with how the word "potential" is unique from other words, such as "resilience." There is no doubt there is at least some overlap between the two terms. However, I see resilience as having the ability to bounce or spring back from difficulty, whereas potential refers to *how far* a person can grow from that challenge. The word "resilience," or bouncing *back*, can imply homeostasis (returning to normal) or status quo.

"Resilience" research initially focused on helping individuals cope with potentially traumatic events (PTEs), but in a welcomed attempt to promote resiliency among all people in all events, being resilient now more commonly refers to any person showing any ability to cope with stress. Instead of noteworthy responses to moments of great stress, it is more and more likely to point to a healthy or normal response to stress.

To further consider the differences between terms, let's examine a study by Anthony Mancini and George Bonanno from Colombia University. In their article, "Resilience in the face of potential trauma: Clinical practices and illustrations," published in the Journal of Clinical Psychology in 2006, they stated that the resilience among individuals who lose a loved one to death is, not only common, but very likely.

> *Generally, a minority of bereaved people, usually between 10% and 15%, suffer chronic grief symptoms beyond the first year after a major loss. . . In fact, most people do not appear to suffer prolonged or extreme disruptions in functioning, and many appear to evidence a <u>striking absence</u> of dysfunction.*

This article, and others like it, show that more often than not, individuals are able to cope, manage, and "get through" life. They are resilient. But the larger or more relevant question is: "Has the loss provided a mechanism and motivation for developing their potential?"

Despite my reservations outlined for the resilience literature, I am one of its biggest fans. It has done a great deal of good, and it is a word and movement that resonates with a wide audience. Perhaps the concept of "bouncing forward," as noted in the David Feldman and Lee Kravetz's book, *SuperSurvivor*, is an attempt to reconnect the concept of resilience to the concept of one's potential after experiencing trauma or loss.

Others may question whether there is any difference between the words "loss," "pain," and "stress." Loss may refer to an actual event, such as when the disability or death occurred, but it more often refers to a state of feeling lost or being "at a loss" for what to do or where to go in life after a traumatic event. This secondary definition of "loss" is then comparable to "stress" and "pain," but "loss" also seems to reflect the reason for that stress and pain, and it is more specific than the words *stress* and *pain*.

Others may wonder what the difference is between the "Value" stage and the word "self-esteem." My response is that self-esteem has become a catch-all term for how a person feels about themselves, whereas "Value" refers to a combination of cognitive and emotional assessments of what one is and how they feel about that assessment. (More detail was also given in the chapter about "Value"). I envision the word "Value" to be comparable to self-concept or "identity."

Early on for my research for this book, the primary question was whether loss victims and survivors experienced or witnessed the "needs" and "potential" aspects of my new framework (i.e. safety, influence, value, investment, and acceptance). While I initially felt the framework would be useful to at least some degree, looking back after all the interviews and research were complete, I admit I was surprised how well it applied to those I interviewed.

Still, if I had the research to do all over again, I would have added more objective data in order to examine whether certain "potential" themes were more applicable among certain groups of people than others. Objectivity is the ability to interpret what we see without letting our values or beliefs affect that interpretation; to that end, I plead guilty. What has been shared with me has had a profound impact on me.

In academia, I feel our focus is too often drawn to finding fault with families and individuals. Like a medical doctor, the emphasis seems to be with identifying what's wrong with others in order to fix them. I believe there is a place for this, but it is often less useful than helping families and individuals recognize their strengths, and to build upon those strengths to help them cope and manage their loss and stress. I encourage academia to more fully recognize the value and expertise of those they study, and to recognize that those who are "stake-holders" in the process and outcome have much to share and teach.

Interviewees (for this book) were selected based on their willingness to share their stories of tragedy, and just as importantly, if they were able to relate how they successfully moved from a point of pain and hopelessness to one of greater potential. Retrospective accounts from those who found a path toward improvement and those who are currently "stuck" in their despair may have very different perspectives of what is needed for individual growth; future research may want to examine to what extent the Potential Framework addresses these different experiences among those who have not overcome or placed their loss in a healthy context.

Most of my interviews were conducted over the phone, and there are some of whom I am unsure of their age, socioeconomic status, and ethnicities. Even among those I have known personally or well, I have sometimes chosen to limit specificities with regard to ethnicity and other information (such as city where they live or changing their names) to provide them with some privacy; many wanted to share their stories, but not at the expense of having their names, details of their trauma, and other descriptors printed in the pages of this book.

It may also be apparent that, when using the Potential Framework, a particular symptom may not be associated with just one need or level. For example, someone who has an eating disorder may want to improve their body, and in the process, feel safe when being seen as beautiful by her peers. Another may have an eating disorder because she sees it as a way of having influence or control (over her body) in her world that seems completely out of control, or be in a family that is controlling of her. Another may experiment with starvation and feel a sense of value with all the positive comments (e.g. "Have you lost weight? You look great!") she gets from her peers. Of course, it should be mentioned that the Potential Framework, as it is written in this book, is theoretical, and it is up to the practitioner and client to determine its worth in their practice.

NOTES

Feldman, D. & Kravetz, L. (2014). *Supersurvivors: The surprising link between suffering and success.* New York: HarperWave.

Mancini, A. & Bonanno, G. (2006). Resilience in the Face of Potential Trauma: Clinical Practices and Illustrations, *Journal of Clinical Psychology, 62(8)*, 971–985.

My Thoughts are Free. See http://en.wikipedia.org/wiki/Die_Gedanken_sind_frei Link accessed August 14, 2014.

Chapter 11: Help and Hope

Beyond one's immediate social or familial circle, there is a wide range of options available for those who need help. There are many types of therapists and counselors, such as marriage and family therapists, psychologists, psychiatrists, addiction recovery counselors, and more. If you are looking for additional help, find a professional who, not only is effective at what they do, but also shares (or at least supports) the values you have.

There are also medical options, such as visiting with a doctor and considering medications that may help balance the mind, or consulting with a nutritionist for the goal of healing the mind and body. One of the individuals I was impressed with when I first considered "loss" was Dr. Daniel Amen, an accomplished author and brain expert, who relies largely on brain scans and nutritional supplements to heal the brain from the inside out.

There are also what many consider non-traditional approaches, although they are becoming more and more common every year. Meditation, hypnosis, and yoga are all examples of learning to focus on relaxing the body, allowing the person to gain more control over their body, mind, and health. Meditation is much harder than expected because it requires the person to listen to and control their own thoughts. Being "present," being in the here and now, or not allowing your thoughts to stray, is a challenge for many of us. One study even found that, when given the option of being shocked or being in a room by oneself without any other person, activity, or technology for 15 minutes, individuals (and especially men) often preferred the shock.

A life coach may be able to help you focus on your spirituality, goal setting, and relationships, all with the intent of helping you reach your potential. One of my expert interviews was with Patrick Wanis, who as a life coach, explained his technique for working with individuals who have experienced loss. The technique is called the Subconscious Rapid Transformation Technique (SRTT), and he trains practitioners how to use it with others. The process should only be employed by a trained and trusted professional, and it involves about an hour and half of going back into one's childhood to find the source of trauma and validating the inner child's emotional and behavioral reaction to that trauma.

Although Patrick Wanis was not familiar with my conception or framework for Potential, nor was I familiar with his perspective before I wrote this book, his approach seems to overlap with my framework by addressing the needs of safety, trust, validation, and forgiveness. He further explained to me that the ultimate goal is to instill a sense of hope, which motivates change and action.

For financial reasons, as well as other reasons, instead of turning to professional help, many turn to family, friends, and clergy when they need help dealing with difficult times. Some people just need to talk out what they have experienced, or to know they are not alone in what happened to them. There are various support groups in-person, as well as online support forums for a variety of loss experiences; typically they are free or low-cost. Before attending or signing up, know all you can about how they can protect your identity.

Again, be cautious about being "willing to try anything" or "miracle cures," which are tempting when going through loss. Take the time, if possible, to consider what types of support would be right for you, your values, your needs, and your finances. Take the time to consider the rewards and risks for each approach, and expect concrete answers on what it will take to get to where you want to be.

NOTES

Khan, A. (July 3, 2014). People left alone with their thoughts choose electric shock. LA Times. http://www.latimes.com/science/sciencenow/la-sci-sn-people-alone-thoughts-mind-dislike-electric-shocks-20140703-story.html Link accessed August 14, 2014.

Chapter 12: Conclusion

Where we are able to go in life, whether in the presence or absence of loss, is determined by how dedicated we are to increasing and living up to our potential. We don't need to be a superstar, popular, or rich to reach our potential. We just have to be willing and committed to doing what it takes. Just ask Barry Adkins.

Just days after his son's death from alcohol poisoning, Barry decided he was going to honor his son, Kevin's, life by walking from Arizona to Montana, a 1400 mile journey. Getting sponsors and getting in shape for such a trek isn't easy, but he was committed to his cause, taking along with him the ashes from his son's body, as both a reminder and companionship in his thoughts and grieving process. Barry also became a motivational speaker and author of *Kevin's Last Walk*. What kept Barry going was the knowledge, given to him in a spiritual way from his son, Kevin, that "something very good will come from this." Just like Barry, whether something very good will come from our tragedies or even in our day-to-day lives is determined by what we choose to do with our loss experiences.

While we seek out and reach up for our potential, it is not a one-time accomplishment. Or as some would say, a "one and done deal." With every new person, situation, emotion, and challenge, we ask ourselves what is possible, acceptable, and ideal. Potential isn't perfection, but it is a process that is perfect for each of us. Potential never makes us better than or above another person, but it does make us better than we were.

If you appreciate someone's positive influence in your life, value their friendship, or recognize their investment in your life or work, please let them know. A compliment not only makes them feel better about themselves, it may actually meet a specific need of theirs, and in the process, help them reach their potential.

Helping Others Reach Their Potential

One of the loneliest paths is the one where you do not have anyone who will encourage you to "have your best day ever." If you are that person, become that person you need. Develop the capacity to self-motivate and hold yourself accountable for reaching your potential, and it will help you increase the potential of others.

I would be grateful if reading this book benefits you with how you view your loss, but be careful that you do not make your loss your entire life. There is so much more to living. If you have lost a loved one to death, you will honor their memory by living more fully rather than remaining in a life centered on loss. If your loss centers on hurt feelings or how you were mistreated, continually reminiscing about it is nothing more than honoring that experience and memory. Your pain does not define the whole you. How you react to it does. If you have experienced loss, learn from it. Even experience the pain from it if you need to. But realize there is much more to life than that loss. Your potential is waiting for you.

Chapter 13: Epilogue

When I began writing this book, I envisioned it being about people who struggled with loss and how they coped. I soon realized that the real story was with how we can use that pain or loss in a way to strengthen ourselves and others. I planned on keeping my own experiences of loss hidden. But the book had other ideas. I felt that for this book to hold integrity, I had to share my own story of loss.

When I'm asked to introduce myself, I typically say I'm married, have three children, and work as a professor in Family and Consumer Sciences at the university. I give a snapshot of who I am, and I take pride in that description. But like others who have experienced loss, I sometimes want to shout a little about my own loss, knowing it has largely defined who I really am. I want my loss to be validated.

There is much to my childhood that I appreciate. Growing up on a farm, I learned the value of hard work, commitment, and responsibility. My parents never divorced, and I was active in sports, excelled in school, and won several talent shows playing the piano and singing in my early years. Life was good.

My mom was the picture of a traditional nurturer. She was there for everything and for every one of her six biological and two foster kids. She spent countless hours cleaning the house while playing a song about how motherhood is a "high and noble call." She played it over, and over, and over again. She also (literally) slept with one eye open, and there were more than dozens of times when that image would freak us out enough to behave, at least when we were still at home.

But there were times when she got angry. That piercing eye, or worse, when she told me, "I'm disappointed in what you just did." Fortunately, those times were rare and minor compared to the moments when she made me feel like I was worth a million bucks. When I was 8-years-old, my finger had been cut off by a barn door as I flew through it pretending to be superhero. After some discussion, panic, and a call to the local ambulance, my parents decided it would be best if they drove me to the hospital located 30 minutes away from our home. While my dad drove, my mom held me and asked if I wanted to pray. I quickly shook my head "no," and replied, "I don't think I can." So she prayed, and the most amazing feeling of peace came over my whole body. There I was, certain I was going to bleed to death, and I wasn't afraid.

Dad taught us to respect and appreciate Mom. Each day, when leaving for school, we would give her a hug and a kiss. As we got older, it seemed a little compulsory, but none of us complained too much. Discipline was common, and ranged everywhere from grounding, putting our hands up as high as long as we could, eating cayenne pepper when saying bad words, and spankings.

Honestly, everything seemed normal. But it wasn't. My mom developed breast cancer in my early childhood years. Dad promised us that if we just "lived right," Mom would be healed.

One day, after our congregation prayed, Mom went back in for a checkup and her cancer had completely disappeared. Our faith had been renewed and strengthened, and the doctors were stunned.

Unfortunately, some time later Mom got cancer again, and we were again promised that if we just lived right, she would be healed again. In my boyish mind, it all seemed logical. It worked the first time, so why wouldn't it work again?

It wasn't until about two weeks before her passing, or when she was taken to the hospital the last time, that I realized, deep within my gut, that she would not live. I remember my brother, ten years older than me, getting ready to drive to the hospital while I remained at home, asking me if I was okay. I nodded yes, but I knew better. I was completely sick. The family eventually decided to bring Mom home from the hospital, and her parents came to visit, only to have one of them experience a heart attack. With stress and its impact, they decided the best thing to do was for them to reluctantly take the 12 hour drive back home.

For some reasons still unknown to me, Dad assigned me (14-years-old at the time, and the second to the youngest of six children) to go with my grandparents to ensure their safety. I packed my things, and as I walked down the hallway, taking me out of sight of my Mom, I heard her scream, "No-o-o-o!" over and over. It is a scream that still haunts me to this day. I was confident it would be the last I would ever hear from her.

After two weeks of spending time at my grandparents, I caught a train ride, arriving home late at night. Early the next morning, Mom passed away.

The loss of that relationship was bad enough. I had lost someone who believed in me, cheered loudly for me, expected great things of me, and had incredible patience with me. I was safe, had influence, and knew I had value in her sight. This is true even when I didn't *want* those things, or was embarrassed by how spiritual or motherly she was. Motherhood was never anything she took lightly.

It's said that you can never fully appreciate someone until they're gone. The first Mother's Day after Mom died, I sat in church while everyone got up to talk about how wonderful their mothers were. There was a pain so severe I thought I was going to explode. I stood up, went outside, opened my car door, and sat in the driver's seat. A few minutes later, my younger brother came and sat in the passenger' seat. There we were, two young men, 15 and 10 years of age, saying nothing, staring out the window for nearly an hour until the meeting was over. We knew nothing about being able to talk about our pain, and no one to show us how.

After the death of Mom, Dad usually hid behind his closed bedroom door, and to my knowledge he never received any government welfare even though he was rarely employed. The cupboards, our refrigerator, and our lives were bare. We starved on so many levels. There is even an anecdotal story of my younger brother walking to a neighbor's house and crying when they offered him a plain slice of bread. I had no idea how to react to others who had even a slight interest in visiting me at my home, but I did everything in my power to keep them from visiting my house, feeling completely ashamed for how bad things were.

I realize now that much of that shame was camouflaged in a cloak of abandonment. My mother had left, my father was unavailable, our cupboards were bare, and the utmost abandonment was that God had deserted me. I no longer lived in a just world, and could not depend on anything or anyone anymore. I thought He had broken my life, my family, my heart, and His promise to me that if I just lived "right," that everything would be okay. But it wasn't okay. Life was no longer fair or hopeful, and at the center of those newly found beliefs was the recognition that I was alone and not worth others "being there" for me. But I couldn't tell anyone. I had always been taught to respond appropriately when someone asked, "How are you?" *I'm fine*, I'd say. I lied.

Earlier in this book, I referenced two teen friends who experienced the loss of a parent, one who seemed to fall apart and the other who was resilient. One of those teens, the one who fell apart, was actually me, and I always wondered what exactly precipitated my friend's ability to be resilient while I was falling to pieces. He had lost his dad, the primary breadwinner in his family, my friend had asthma, and he had been held back a grade. He definitely had his share of loss experiences. A few years later, in his early adult years, he lost his mother to cancer.

I look back on that comparison between his response to trauma and mine and see the Potential Framework written all over it. He had his physical needs taken care of (Safety).

He was not afraid to speak his mind (Influence). He started on a basketball team and felt connected to the community (Value), and he had a strong band of siblings who worked together on a farm to provide income (Investment).

Of the limited interaction I had with my dad, much of the dialog had to do with him asking me to pray for things I was uncomfortable praying for. They were definitely things that were outside the bounds of what I thought was moral or ethical. And his comments or teasing, although seemingly playful at first, coupled with a lack of positive attention or having my needs met, caused me a great deal of pain. He often laughed at me while I drove on rural, dirt roads and how bumpy it seemed to him in the passenger seat, and he chuckled at things I did or didn't do. *There was only one bump in the road and you hit it. Do you ever think you'll amount to a hill of beans? Your writing is so bad, someday I bet you'll become a doctor.*

But the hardest part, what hurt me the most, was when he went into his room, closed and locked the door, and seldom come out to see his children. It happened nearly every day, and nearly all day. Once when I tried to read his journal, which I knew would reveal why he seldom came outside his room, he slapped my cheek so hard I thought my head would fall off. I knew reading another person's journal was incredibly wrong, but I felt I had a right to know why my life was the way it was.

A couple years prior, when I was about 12, and just a couple years before mom died, he took me outside and told me he was going to beat me until I learned my lesson. It was so random. I was in shock, terrified, and confused. I

176

hadn't done anything wrong, and I had no clue why I should be punished, let alone in the way he detailed. After repeated pleadings and questioning what I had done, his only response was that I needed to shut up and learn my lesson. What was the lesson, I kept asking. You're just going to learn it, he replied. With my voice quaking, I looked him in the eyes and cried, "This is wrong and you know it!" I then walked away, with my legs feeling like they were going to give out on me, and wondering if he would attack me from behind. Ironically, even though I look back on this experience and see the courage of a 12-year-old boy, my perception of that experience at the time was that I must have done something wrong. I understand now that experience, coupled with other experiences, made me completely afraid of violence.

During my teen years, I was known for smiling a lot, but I held on to a troubling secret. I could no longer stand up for myself. I had been abandoned, and I was no longer worth fighting for. I knew that if I let my anger out, that I may seriously hurt someone. I had to keep it in check. Over time, this secret of not defending myself became more and more exposed as I received constant bullying from a few individuals in my school. (One of these high school bullies even found me when I went to college, hundreds of miles away from my home, and he gathered a group of guys to taunt and harass me). Despite being on my high school varsity athletic teams and being overall well-liked (i.e. I was voted "Most Friendly" in my senior class), I felt others were losing respect in me, and I in myself.

I often screamed at myself, "What is wrong with you? Just hit back! Do something!" It wasn't the fear of getting hurt so much as the fear of what else might happen in my life if I didn't live right; in my mind at the time, all conflict was evil, and if I defended myself, I would only be promoting more conflict. I seesawed back and forth from being mad at God (and everyone else) for "taking" my mom when I had been living right, to assuming it must've been my fault that my mom died. Ironically, I wasn't afraid to stand up for others, but still I struggled to stand up for myself. I figured if God, my mom, and my dad deserted me, I didn't deserve to be protected. I wasn't worth it.

Finally, and in my late teen years, I'd had enough, and started confronting those who should have kept me safe, who should have allowed me to share my voice, and who should have let me know I was of value. In my heart, I felt I would someday prove to them I was of value. That moment, and others like it, sparked a belief in me that I had potential, and I began to change how I saw myself. As I've started my own family, I have learned to create boundaries to protect those I love and confront the self-destructive beliefs and memories from my childhood.

Despite the horror of my childhood memories, with many left unshared, there were some good memories too. One day my dad approached me, a few months before my 18th birthday, and asked if I thought about earning my Eagle Scout award. The award, which must be earned before a boy's 18th birthday, was the furthest from my mind. I had actually given up earning it after my mom died (when I was 14 years old).

Something about dad's question stayed with me, and I ended up defying everyone's expectations by earning the award just a couple days before my 18th birthday. It was a major turning point in my life, a symbol of hope and control over my circumstances.

I also remember how much my dad loved my mom. He stayed by her side for large amounts of time, each day, over a space of years, looking to give her comfort. He made sure her children treated her "right," which usually meant no talking back, and to give her a kiss before we left for school. I also knew that Dad's compassion was extended to me from my earliest years, when I was born, as he fasted (going without food) for three full days, petitioning God to heal me from a collapsed lung.

Someone must have known a little about my home life during my early teen years after Mom died, because eventually I was asked if I wanted to work at the high school cafeteria in exchange for "free" lunches. Neither I nor anyone I talked to had heard of a student helping in the lunchroom before. It didn't help me win popularity points, but I knew I had to eat. And eat I did, as I was able to get extra "everything" by working there, and I banked on those calories to last for the next 24 hours.

In my teen years, whenever I could, I took additional employment to pay for food, sports, and dates. I moved irrigation lines or pipe, sprayed and planted asparagus, moved Post Office furniture, helped deliver appliances, and even worked at a chicken farm. I prided myself on being a hard worker, but I knew I had to do something different to escape the life I was living.

I want to make it clear that what I am sharing is not intended for shock value, to get anyone's sympathy, or even to sell an extra book. I'm a very private person, and I usually do not share things like this. In all honestly, I do not like sharing any personal information, but if there is any moment when you are wondering if the author has experienced loss, or has some real life expertise outside of research, then it is here for you to gauge. What I share is not about getting justice or revenge. I've made my fair share of mistakes too.

These unmet needs, and my desperation for meeting them, served as self-fulfilling prophecies for disaster, especially in relationships. I objectified people, seeing them as merely things to serve my needs; if they did not meet those needs, I felt I had no use for them.

I share my message with you, realizing now that all those experiences are a piece of who I am, for better and worse. I am more compassionate than I would have been. I am more helpful to those in need because of my own experiences. I am also very creative, looking to make something positive out of something difficult or painful. I am passionate about improving the lives of those who are oppressed, particularly within family relationships. I am also a little broken, at times, by those memories of pain. I know those memories have an impact on what and how I think, and they can also impact those I love the most.

Even today, when I sometimes feel the need to talk about the loss in my life, I see skepticism, avoidance, and this, "You seriously should be over that by now" or "Be a man" look in the eyes of others. I don't blame those who do not want to listen to me about my loss. It can be very awkward to listen to.

When I was 18 years old, I asked my Dad, "Why haven't you ever talked about your dad?" All he told me was, "I was glad when my dad died." I don't know what my dad's life was like as a child, but I know he must have experienced loss too, even though much of it was left unspoken, because it had an enormous impact on me. My wife often tells me that hurt people hurt people, and for my teen years, the limited interaction that took place within the walls of my house taught me I would never amount to anything. It wouldn't surprise me if his childhood was more traumatizing than mine. And I hope his life is healing.

Fortunately, my story is also about how some people *were* there for me, and who made a positive difference in my life. Without their help, I'm afraid of the path I would have followed.

Without a conscious effort, I too often overlook their kindness and focus on the wrongs perpetuated against me. My siblings, a secretary at my high school, a mother (who I called "mom" for years) of a former girlfriend, my friends, a leader of my church and banker who took me aside and shared the realities of what it takes to provide for a family were among those whom I am grateful for and who literally rescued me. I know there were others, working behind the scenes, but I only know that now, decades later.

Just recently, while writing this book, and nearly 30 years after my mom's death, I heard about individuals who helped my dad get a $50,000 life insurance policy, which in

1985, was a considerable sum of money, paid when Mom died. I also never knew, until recently, of the frequent checks that came in from those who cared about us. I am grateful for their help, and wish I could have known then where the money came from or went to. Our food, clothing, housing, and transportation were all lower than poverty levels, but at least knowing there were kind people provides comfort.

Sometimes I'm asked why I would ever write a book like this. Hearing about loss is usually a very stressful thing for me, but do you want to know what changed that for me? When I listened to others' accounts of loss, I wondered how I could share their stories in a way that would help others. I found myself fulfilling an Investment need, and sharing this book helped me see loss differently than I had before. My personal loss developed new meaning. It's time for you to determine what meaning your loss has for you.